ROUTLEDGE LIBRARY EDITIONS: LIBRARY AND INFORMATION SCIENCE

Volume 44

IMPLEMENTING ONLINE UNION LISTS OF SERIALS

IMPLEMENTING ONLINE UNION LISTS OF SERIALS

The Pennsylvania Union List of Serials Experience

Edited by
RUTH C. CARTER AND JAMES D. HOOKS

LONDON AND NEW YORK

First published in 1989 by The Haworth Press, Inc.

This edition first published in 2020
by Routledge
2 Park Square, Milton Park, Abingdon, Oxon OX14 4RN

and by Routledge
52 Vanderbilt Avenue, New York, NY 10017

Routledge is an imprint of the Taylor & Francis Group, an informa business

© 1989 The Haworth Press, Inc.

All rights reserved. No part of this book may be reprinted or reproduced or utilised in any form or by any electronic, mechanical, or other means, now known or hereafter invented, including photocopying and recording, or in any information storage or retrieval system, without permission in writing from the publishers.

Trademark notice: Product or corporate names may be trademarks or registered trademarks, and are used only for identification and explanation without intent to infringe.

British Library Cataloguing in Publication Data
A catalogue record for this book is available from the British Library

ISBN: 978-0-367-34616-4 (Set)
ISBN: 978-0-429-34352-0 (Set) (ebk)
ISBN: 978-0-367-36136-5 (Volume 44) (hbk)
ISBN: 978-0-367-36141-9 (Volume 44) (pbk)
ISBN: 978-0-429-34411-4 (Volume 44) (ebk)

Publisher's Note
The publisher has gone to great lengths to ensure the quality of this reprint but points out that some imperfections in the original copies may be apparent.

Disclaimer
The publisher has made every effort to trace copyright holders and would welcome correspondence from those they have been unable to trace.

Implementing Online Union Lists of Serials: The Pennsylvania Union List of Serials Experience

Ruth C. Carter
James D. Hooks
Editors

The Haworth Press
New York • London

Implementing Online Union Lists of Serials: The Pennsylvania Union List of Serials Experience is monographic supplement #5 to the journal *The Serials Librarian*. It is not supplied as part of the subscription to the journal, but is available from the publisher at an additional charge.

© 1989 by The Haworth Press, Inc. (except for reprinted articles). All rights reserved. No part of this work may be reproduced or utilized in any form or by any means, electronic or mechanical, including photocopying, microfilm and recording, or by any information storage and retrieval system, without permission in writing from the publisher. Printed in the United States of America.

The following chapters are reprinted:

Steps Toward an On-Line Union List and *Pittsburgh Regional Library Center Serials Cancellation Project* (with permission of the American Library Association).
Cataloging Decisions on Pre-AACR2 Serial Records from a Union List Viewpoint (with permission from *Union Lists: Issues and Answers*).
Online Services and Collection Development (with permission from *Serials Review*).
Union Listing—A Tool for Reference Service (with permission from West Virginia Libraries).
Pennsylvania Union List of Serials: Procedure Manual (with permission from the State Library of Pennsylvania).

The Haworth Press, Inc., 12 West 32 Street, New York, NY 10001
EUROSPAN/Haworth, 3 Henrietta Street, London WC2E 8LU England

LIBRARY OF CONGRESS
Library of Congress Cataloging-in-Publication Data

Implementing online union lists of serials : the Pennsylvania union list of serials experience / Ruth C. Carter, James D. Hooks, editors.
    p. cm. — (Monographic supplement #5 to the Serials librarian, ISSN 0897-8409)
    Includes bibliographies and index.
    ISBN 0-86656-802-6
    1. Serials control system—Automation. 2. Catalogs, Union—Automation. 3. Catalogs, On-line. 4. PaULS (Information retrieval system) I. Carter, Ruth C. II. Hooks, James D. III. Title: Implementing on line union lists of serials. IV. Series: Monographic supplement . . . to the Serials librarian : #5.
Z692.S5I55 1988
025.3'432'0285—dc19   88-24303
                                                                                         CIP

CONTENTS

Introduction
      Ruth C. Carter, MA, MS
      James D. Hooks, MLS, PhD
	1

The Pennsylvania Union List of Serials: A Macroview *Ruth C. Carter, MA, MS*	3

The Pennsylvania Union List of Serials: Initial Development
      Ruth C. Carter, MA, MS
      Scott Bruntjen, MA, MS, DA
	9

The Pennsylvania Union List of Serials: Continuing Development
      Ruth C. Carter, MA, MS
      Scott Bruntjen, MA, MA, DA
	19

The Pennsylvania Union List of Serials: From Development to Maintenance
      Ruth C. Carter, MA, MS
      Scott Bruntjen, MA, MA, DA
	31

The Pennsylvania Union List of Serials: Maintenance and Beyond
      Ruth C. Carter, MA, MS
      James D. Hooks, MLS, PhD
	47

Steps Toward an On-Line Union List *Ruth C. Carter, MA, MS*	61

Cataloging Decisions on Pre-AACR2 Serials Records
from a Union List Viewpoint   73
    Ruth C. Carter, MA, MS

Pittsburgh Regional Library Center Serials Cancellation
Project   77
    Ruth C. Carter, MA, MS
    Scott Bruntjen, MA, MA, DA

Online Services and Collection Development   89
    Ruth C. Carter, MA, MS

Union Listing – A Tool for Reference Service   97
    James D. Hooks, MLS, PhD

West Virginia Union List – A Need Fulfilled   107
    Mildred Moyers, MA, MLS

PaULS Participation by a Special Library   119
    Betty P. Schwarz, MS, MLS

Serial Union Listing in a Regional Academic Consortium   129
    Susan A. Cady, MLS, MPA

PaULS: A View from the Network   141
    Rian Miller-McIrvine, MM, MLS

Annotated Bibliography on Online Union Lists of Serials,
1979-1987   159
    James D. Hooks, MLS, PhD

Pennsylvania Union List of Serials: Procedure Manual
(2nd Edition)   193
    Suzanne L. Thomas, MA
    Henrietta F. Angus, MLS
    Alice Bright, MLS
        Editors

Index   219

Introduction

Each of us has worked with the Pennsylvania Union List of Serials (PaULS) in a variety of capacities for almost a decade. Our collective experience with online union listing precedes the establishment of PaULS as both of us were involved with at least one of its predecessors — the union lists of serials of the University of Pittsburgh and the Pittsburgh Regional Library Center.

This book attempts to collect the previously published articles recording the development and implementation of PaULS; provide new articles representing the viewpoints and experiences of several participants and Palinet, the network giving service to libraries in eastern Pennsylvania; make available the PaULS procedure manual; and include an annotated bibliography of literature about online union listing. The participants' articles describe the extensive union listing activities of West Virginia University; a special library, Calgon Corporation; and a regional consortia, the Lehigh Valley Association of Independent Colleges.

The introductory essay gives a broad view of PaULS and the environment in which it was developed and implemented, and is now maintained. To assist others in using online union lists of serials, this book includes an annotated bibliography of publications related to online union lists of serials and the newly revised Pennsylvania Union List of Serials Procedure Manual. Although PaULS is OCLC based, the general lessons that can be learned from this book, it is felt, should have wide application.

We hope that this book will be of value and interest both to those specifically interested in online union lists of serials and those who are interested in the record of a large cooperative undertaking, especially one involved in building and maintaining a database.

PaULS would not have been possible without the foresight and hard work of many people. With continued commitment, it can be of service for many more years.

Ruth C. Carter
James D. Hooks

The Pennsylvania Union List of Serials: A Macroview

Ruth C. Carter, MA, MS

SUMMARY. This essay provides an overview of the Pennsylvania Union List of Serials (PaULS) in the context of the conditions and times in which it developed. The evolution of important factors in the development and implementation of online union lists of serials is noted. PaULS is entering a period that should bring emphasis to maintenance and applications rather than to file building.

The union lists of serials of the University of Pittsburgh and Pennsylvania have occupied a significant fraction of this author's professional time during almost a decade and a half. Most of that period has seen a continuous, dramatic evolution in union listing including the transition from batch mode update of tapes to online updates; from printed lists either in hard copy or microform to access to the union list in electronic form via shared online databases; from skeletal bibliographic information to holdings tied to serial records cataloged in accordance with full national standards. To put it briefly – the times have been exciting, the challenges substantial, and the results rewarding.

Many of the articles in this book contain a record of the author's union listing activities. They cover the period before the formal initiation of the Pennsylvania Union List of Serials (PaULS) to the development and evolution of PaULS. Although, there is no need to redescribe what has already been recorded, it seems appropriate to review at a mega level what has happened, describe relevant issues and trends at present, and speculate on the future of large-scale cooperative online union lists of serials.

In 1973 OCLC purchased the union list tapes of the Pittsburgh Regional Library Center (PRLC) and the University of Pittsburgh (Pitt). Those two serial union lists were selected as a base for loading bibliographic records for serials into the OCLC online union catalog for several reasons including: size of the files, machine readability, and amount of bibliographic data in the records. In the late 1980s with the benefit of over a decade of CONSER activity, it is difficult to remember that a demand for typical brief union list records ever existed.

Shortly after OCLC purchased the Pitt and PRLC serial tapes, the Minnesota Union List of Serials (MULS) became available. MULS had the advantage of MARC tags and more bibliographic data. Consequently, OCLC first devoted time to programming the conversion of the MULS records. The PRLC and Pitt records were not entered into the OCLC database until 1976. CONSER was already several years old and the OCLC users were conditioned to more bibliographic data more accurately tagged than that loaded from the Pitt and PRLC tapes. This led to the Pitt staff's initiating a period of intensive cleanup of the University's records online.

Although CONSER records strove for completeness, a number of compromises on standards were made initially. The chief compromise was acceptance of input of records using latest entry cataloging. Initially it was agreed that the Library of Congress would use successive entry cataloging only for titles that began publication after 1971. This became an area of considerable frustration.

Many contributors to the OCLC database, including some union list groups, preferred that all records be in successive entry. The AACR2 cataloging rules called for successive entry. Medical libraries not only used title main entry but preferred successive entry because of the form of citation a user would probably have. OCLC's policy was that all new records and current cataloging be in accordance with current rules and standards. Eventually, the Library of Congress and CONSER adopted successive entry as a requirement.

Another area of contention was that of multiple bibliographic items for the same intellectual work. In union lists this came out particularly in the issue of display of holdings of hard copy and microformat for the same title. OCLC held to its official position of separate bibliographic records for separate formats as both AACR2 and the holdings standard specified separate bibliographic records. Nonetheless, the OCLC Serials Control Advisory Committee and union list participants urged that an exception to the policy be permitted.

Many union list groups in the early 1980s adopted the exception policy. Pennsylvania did not. The primary rationale was that it would be easier to put together separate records than to take apart single records. Although it was recognized that users would prefer all holdings for a title connected to one bibliographic entity, there were other considerations, including use of a shared bibliographic record for acquisition purposes.

In the last several years the PaULS policy to use separate records for each format has been relaxed. Several factors entered into that policy change. One factor is the adoption by the United States Newspaper Program of the "master record concept," whereby all holdings and the basic bibliographic description are based on the hard copy, even though the only extant version of the newspaper may be in microform. Other considerations included the continuing concern of public services staff with making holdings displays both simpler and more comprehensive for users. In addition, there were economic issues. A minor concern was the additional cost of online storage and either offline or online display of multiple entries. The cost of creation of the bibliographic record for a microformat was more significant.

At the same time that standards connected to input of data into union lists evolved, OCLC strengthened its commitment to quality control and a clean database. In recent years many records have been deleted from the OCLC online union catalog. This, combined with new search qualifiers for serials, microformats, and dates, make it much less difficult to select records to use for union listing. The new search strategies available from within the Serials Control Subsystem also help achieve precision in searching and identification of the record for a particular title already in use by a given union list group.

Selection of records and searching were two important topics in the original PaULS manual published in 1982. The improvements in searching were a motivating factor in the decision to prepare a

2nd edition. Just completed in 1987, the *Pennsylvania Union List of Serials Procedure Manual*, 2nd edition, is offered as part of this publication.

As we enter a second decade of online union listing, there is a noticeable transition in focus from development and file building to maintenance and applications. Nobody has ever suggested that maintenance of anything was glamorous, much less easy. Union listing is no exception. But, applications are what union listing or any other file building effort are all about. It seems clear that in terms of youth, maturity, and old age of online databases, applications are part of maturity. Because emphasis on applications is, to this author, in an early stage, it can be considered that union lists of serials, as represented by the Pennsylvania Union List of Serials, have reached the stage of shifting emphasis from just building the database to deciding now that the database is available, how to use it most effectively. In that light, PaULS is probably in early maturity.

The developers of PaULS, including this author, were among those who realized that a large serials database would make possible many applications. Work included a pilot project funded by the Council on Library Resources to investigate use of an online serials database to communicate collection management information, especially information about serial titles selected for cancellation. It was recognized that this application could readily extend to titles selected for acquisition as well as those being considered for either cancellation or acquisition.

Other possible applications include: expanding the traditional areas of resource sharing to cooperative storage and/or preservation of serials; analysis of overlap or collection strength among several institutions; and use of expanded bibliographic records for decision-making purposes. An example of the latter is using the indexing and abstracting fields to make collection development decisions based on the possibility of users having citations to particular serials.

Inclusion of abstracting and indexing coverage has been part of the CONSER Program's shift to applications. Like individual union lists, the CONSER Program (Cooperative Online Serials Program) has redefined its emphasis from file building to maintenance and applications. The CONSER Retreat in the fall of 1986 resulted in a restatement of CONSER's goals and objectives. Encouraging and facilitating use of the massive CONSER file is a priority.

At this point in time it is difficult to project the future of PaULS or any other specific online union list of serials. Many of the original driving factors in the establishment of PaULS still exist including: to bring together in one source the many small union lists existing throughout Pennsylvania, make the resources of smaller institutions more widely known in order to spread out use of collections, and have current holdings information for serial resources widely available on a timely basis. However, other circumstances have changed.

Two areas of concern among online union list participants using OCLC are copyright release and record use. Much of the work involved in file building of serial bibliographic and holdings records was funded with federal or state money. Any attempt by OCLC to impose restraints that would limit good faith use of government funded data entry could make funding bodies hesitate to further support a particular union list's maintenance via OCLC. PaULS encountered this problem when the State Library of Pennsylvania hoped to include PaULS as one portion of a CD-ROM disk containing other Library Services and Construction Act (LSCA) funded records. From this author's point of view, distribution of PaULS holdings to offline as well as online users can only encourage additional maintenance of the PaULS database. Union list groups or other entities building their databases through a utility are well advised to consider possible uses and applications prior to initiating file building. There is definitely a need for planning in this area so that participating libraries or other institutions can protect themselves and their rights to future use of the databases they build or fund.

A second factor in the future of PaULS and other online union lists is the development of local automated library systems. As more libraries implement local online catalogs, the capacity for several libraries in a given region to share access to a common database is increased. The linked systems project and other work being done to have disparate systems speak to each other will also accelerate sharing access on local and regional levels. There will undoubtedly be pressure from administrators to concentrate efforts on cooperative ventures in the smaller area. A vision of the more broad-based contribution to meeting the needs of users on a national, even international, basis must exist if entities such as PaULS are to continue to thrive.

In order for administrators to make the necessary commitments to maintenance of a large-scale online union list such as PaULS, it is necessary for them to have a sense of its value. Reference and interlibrary loan librarians must provide feedback on its usefulness. Collection development librarians should be trained to use the records to the fullest—both in terms of understanding fields in the bibliographic record, such as the 510 tag containing indexing and abstracting coverage, and in terms of taking advantage of acquisition or de-acquisition information included with holdings records.

Although there is room to augment the number of titles within the scope of CONSER, the United States Newspaper Program is likely to represent the last massive effort in the basic file-building stage. Assuming a reasonable commitment of most participants to maintenance, the excitement of the immediate future of online union lists, including PaULS, belongs to those who devise ways to manipulate and take advantage of the data.

The period of maturity of PaULS and other large online union lists of serials should last into the last decade of the twentieth century. Whether they will reach old age (little use or maintenance) by the time the twenty-first century arrives is difficult to predict. However, it is certain that the need to connect users with information published in serials will continue. Either PaULS in its present form or its equivalent will exist in the years ahead.

The Pennsylvania Union List of Serials: Initial Development

Ruth C. Carter, MA, MS
Scott Bruntjen, MA, MS, DA

SUMMARY. The Pennsylvania Union List of Serials is a new project funded by the State Library of Pennsylvania. In 1979 it awarded the Pittsburgh Regional Library Center $99,304 in LSCA Title III funds for first year development of a statewide union list which will be on-line through OCLC. PRLC's history of working with on-line union lists is reviewed, and plans for the first year are described. Initially, there will be concentration on system design. At the same time, a core list of approximately 2,000 titles will be selected, as will the libraries to participate during 1979-1980. Future plans will consider some decentralization and COM production. All work will be in accordance with national standards and plans. The Pennsylvania Union List of Serials will incorporate the PRLC and University of Pittsburgh on-line union lists, which already have data for more than 50,000 titles and 150,000 holdings on-line. This project should work to bring uniformity and fairness to interlibrary loan lending and borrowing throughout the state.

INTRODUCTION

The Pennsylvania Union List of Serials is the outgrowth of the need for a comprehensive, current, an readily searchable tool for the location of serial holdings data within the state. This need, present for many years, was documented clearly in the study *Bibliographic Access in Pennsylvania* (BAS).[1] That study, completed in

---

Scott Bruntjen is Executive Director, Pittsburgh Regional Library Center, Chatham College, Pittsburgh, PA 15232. He is also Project Administrator, Pennsylvania Union List of Serials.
Reprinted from *The Serials Librarian*, Vol. 5(3), Spring 1981.

1979, was funded by the State Library of Pennsylvania and was conducted under the auspices of the Pittsburgh Regional Library Center (PRLC) and the Pennsylvania Area Library Network (PA-LINET).

A major concern of the State Library was for steps to be taken to lessen the imbalance within Pennsylvania between interlibrary loan net borrowers and net lenders. At the same time, it was interested in minimizing the need for utilization of resources outside Pennsylvania.

Librarians in Pennsylvania in response to the survey taken for the BAS often cited the need for a statewide union list as a major area for action. Although many individual union lists could be found in the state, they varied in completeness, coverage, distribution, format, and currency. The lack of up-to-date information was considered a special issue, and the desirability of an on-line union list emerged as an obvious goal. However, as some libraries in Pennsylvania do not have OCLC terminals and probably will not, the BAS proposed that a statewide union list also be available in computer-output microform (COM).

The BAS stated that any statewide list which might be developed should be in accordance with national standards and compatible with the projected National Serials Data Program, which places emphasis on meeting a large percentage of periodical needs at local, state, or regional levels.

After consideration of the Bibliographic Access Study recommendation to develop a statewide on-line union list of serials for Pennsylvania, the State Library of Pennsylvania issued a Request for Proposal (RFP) for that project in May 1979. Responses to the RFP were due no later than July 1, 1979, with work to begin on or about October 1, 1979. The RFP specified that the Pennsylvania Union List be on-line through OCLC and have the capability for microform production. The latter, however, was not to be included in the first year proposal. OCLC was specified because, as the RFP noted, most of the major public and academic libraries and some special libraries have OCLC terminals available for cataloging and interlibrary loan purposes.

PRLC: HISTORICAL BACKGROUND

PRLC was in a favorable position to respond to the RFP. It had a long history of union list activity. More significantly, however, it was engaged on a current basis in development of its union list including that of the University of Pittsburgh on OCLC.

PRLC's on-line union list efforts date back to 1974 when the PRLC union list data base was purchased by OCLC. The contract between PRLC and OCLC specified that OCLC would create bibliographic records and also would load the holdings information from the Pitt and PRLC tapes. The history and design of the PRLC union list activity with OCLC through December 1977 has been described by Carter.[2] By that time the bibliographic records for all PRLC titles had been loaded. Of those, approximately 20,000 were added as records new to the data base. The remainder, approximately 25,000, were found in the previously loaded Minnesota Union List of Serials (MULS) records. In those cases, the Pitt and PRLC symbols were attached to the appropriate MULS record.

The second step was the loading of the holdings information into local data records (LDR). Using repeatable fields within the RTHD (retrospective holdings) field, the Pitt union list data became available on-line in 1977. On February 2, 1980, this important step was completed for PRLC.

Because of the delayed conversion of its holdings data, PRLC could not begin to update that information for titles in the 1973 list. However, PRLC was adding data for titles not in its 1973 union list while Pitt was actively maintaining its union list information on-line at the time the State Library issued its RFP in the spring of 1979. This activity was directed by the Head, Serials Unit, at the University of Pittsburgh, who also served as Chairperson of the PRLC Ad Hoc Committee on the Union List of Periodicals.

This committee was composed of representatives from approximately ten PRLC institutions at any particular time plus a liaison member from the Pittsburgh Chapter of the Special Libraries Association and the PRLC Executive Director ex-officio. A broad-based effort by PRLC, including input from the Union List Committee members who met on this subject in early June 1979, resulted in agreement on basic concepts for the gradual, structured development of a Pennsylvania statewide union list. The PRLC proposal was submitted in mid-July 1979. Official announcement of the acceptance of the PRLC proposal was made in August 1979 by the Acting State Librarian. The contract awarded PRLC was funded by Title III of the Library Services and Construction Act with a budget of $99,304 for the first year running from October 1, 1979 to September 30, 1980.

SCOPE AND DESIGN

Initially, the Pennsylvania Union List of Serials will be developed with a selected group of participating libraries and a core list of approximately 2,000 of the most commonly borrowed serial titles. It was agreed at an early stage that the best chance for effective progress was to structure the activity carefully. Consequently, it was proposed and accepted that efforts in the first year be directed toward systems design prefaced by a thorough state-of-the-art review and toward building on-line holdings data for the 2,000 titles for a limited number of libraries which would be asked to be initial participants. The libraries would be selected carefully to provide geographic distribution within the state and representation of different sizes and types of libraries. Because there is considerable on-line union list work in western Pennsylvania by the University of Pittsburgh and other PRLC area libraries, many of the first participating libraries will be from central or eastern Pennsylvania.

From the outset, a commitment was made to conduct all work in accordance with national standards and plans. These included the recently adopted ANSI Standard for Summary Holding Data and full bibliographic standards represented in AACR, MARC-S, and the CONSER Editing Guide. Because emphasis was to be placed on full bibliographic data, the proposal provided for the possibility of two work sites and for the splitting of activity into bibliographic activities and other union list activities, principally those concerned with holdings data. In order to provide for adequate quality control and completion of first year goals, it was decided to centralize work on the Pennsylvania Union List within the context of two work sites. It was recognized that the possibility of decentralized activity would be explored for the future. Substantial decentralization of input of holdings to the institution level is considered to be fundamental to long-term maintenance of the statewide union list on a current basis. It is thought probable at this time that bibliographic activities will require ongoing central review and action. Moreover, a central union list facility will continue to be required to enter holdings data for libraries in Pennsylvania which do not have OCLC terminals.

ACTIVITIES TO FEBRUARY 2, 1980

One of the first steps of the project staff was to secure the necessary space for the union list central and for the bibliographic activities. The latter is located at the University of Pittsburgh Libraries. This is advantageous because the Serials Cataloger hired for the Pennsylvania Union List will be located in the Pitt Serials Unit, which already has extensive cataloging of serials underway. Space for the union list central office was secured in the same building on the Chatham College campus which presently houses the PRLC headquarters. The two sites are a short distance from each other, with the result that communication problems are minimized. In addition, the project's Technical Director is located at Pitt while the Project Administrator is at PRLC. An OCLC terminal was acquired to support work at each location.

Four full-time positions were provided for in the contract. The Coordinator/Editor began on February 1, 1980, the Serials Cataloger on January 3, 1980. The Project Secretary was the first hired and began on October 29, 1979. The Searcher/Inputter was filled on February 1, 1980. With the exception of the Coordinator/Editor, who was originally planned to be hired by December, all positions have been filled on schedule.

The Coordinator/Editor will have several key responsibilities. These include the development of the core list of titles, the securing the full participation of selected libraries, and the monitoring of the entry of holdings data to ensure consistency and accuracy. Cataloging of titles new to the OCLC data base and decisions related to bibliographical control will be the responsibility of the Serials Cataloger. The CONSER Editing Guide will be used for bibliographic efforts. Some of the time of the Cataloger will be allocated to upgrading bibliographic records for titles in the OCLC data base which were converted from the University of Pittsburgh and PRLC union list records in 1976.

Considerable work has already been done to review these records and delete those which are duplicates of better records from the OCLC data base. It is planned to upgrade all records which are not duplicates as rapidly as permitted by available staff and resources.

Establishment of an Advisory Committee was an important early task. The RFP specified that it should consist of ten persons representing a cross section of Pennsylvania libraries. When the Advisory Committee was formed by the contractor in consultation with the State Library, it was agreed that eight members were to be from within Pennsylvania and that one of these was to be a representative from the State Library. The other two members were to represent national interests and were selected from OCLC, Inc. and the Library of Congress. In addition, the Project Administrator and Technical Director serve in an ex-officio capacity. Two meetings of the Advisory Committee were held in the Fall Quarter of 1979. The Advisory Committee will review plans and provide guidance where needed.

A major effort was made at the outset of this project to bring key staff up-to-date concerning the state of the art of major union list activities. This was accomplished through a number of means: on-site visits to other union list projects, consultant visits, a literature review, correspondence, and telephone communication. At all times, the efforts made in the development of the Pennsylvania Union List of Serials are undertaken with a full commitment toward use of existing bibliographic standards and plans. In order to give this major statewide effort national value this was a key requirement. By sharing information on Pennsylvania plans with others in union list work and by gaining the benefit of their experiences, the project staff believes that users statewide and nationally will be the beneficiaries. Many people in many different states were very generous with their time and data regarding union list developments. The cooperation with which the Pennsylvania Union List of Serials project met is another example of the widespread commitment toward building a national serials data base.

Throughout the course of the project it will be necessary to interact frequently with OCLC. Two topics discussed in the initial period were the conversion of PRLC holdings data from the 1973 union list and the capabilities and constraints of OCLC's new union listing arrangements. Effects of new developments will be closely watched for their impact on current and future PRLC and Pennsylvania union list activities.

One of the early responsibilities of the Project staff will be the development of the core list of titles and the selection of the participating libraries. This delineation of the scope of the titles and libraries to be included is scheduled for the spring of 1980 and was a topic of considerable discussion at the second Advisory Committee meeting. Among the criteria for the inclusion of the core titles will be the coverage of them by abstracting and indexing tools. In addition, interlibrary loan records of serials activity within the state will be surveyed as one method of determining titles that will help make an immediate contribution to meeting needs of the leveling of interlibrary lending and borrowing activity within the state. As was mentioned previously, there will be an attempt to achieve geographic distribution.

PROBLEMS

A major problem at the date of writing this article is that the design for the union list format is not complete and may have to be used in preliminary form for the first year or two. Further, because of outside factors, the initial design will not be decided upon until after further review and until the latest possible date, in March or early April, for the finalization of the data collection forms. The primary factor influencing the timing of design decisions is the pace of union list developments at OCLC, Inc.

For many years OCLC and others have considered the desirability of establishing a union listing capability in the OCLC system. This would be for the specific purposes of providing union list holdings data in a consistent and specialized manner. Although some union listing efforts, including those at Pitt, PRLC, and SUNY, are presently being developed at OCLC, they use the Serials Control

System and fields in the Serials Local Data Record, which were designed with the check-in operation in mind.

A major step toward the accomplishment of a true union listing capability came with the awarding of an HEA Title II-C grant to the Indiana University Libraries to do large-scale retrospective conversion of serials and on-line union listing. Included in the funds for that proposal was a substantial amount for OCLC to do the necessary systems and programming to bring up a specific union list capability. That capability is scheduled to be available in September 1980.

In order to implement the union list capability, OCLC will establish two new fields for summary holdings data meeting ANSI standards. Data for each holding location or copy will be input into separate local data records and displayed together in a union list format. In contrast, the present method used, which was previously described by Carter,[3] consists of use of the RTHD field with repeatable subfields for library, issues held, and dates of coverage.

PRLC has been in close contact with OCLC regarding the status of the union listing capability. Although no final decision has been made, it appears likely that data for the Pennsylvania Union List of Serials will be entered initially into local data records using the existing method. This information will then be readily searchable under the PRLC search-only authorization number. OCLC has acknowledged a commitment to the PRLC union list and has stated that when the new union listing capability is available, it will modify the PRLC data from single records per title to one for each holding location. Therefore, work done in the current mode will not be lost as the OCLC system evolves.

The constraints on design by the OCLC system and its pending new developments are one sort of problem. Another issue, the conversion of the PRLC holdings data as specified in the PRLC/OCLC contract, was eliminated on February 2, 1980 when that portion of the contract was completed by OCLC. With this conversion accomplished, PRLC is now in the process of authorizing the elimination of several hundred duplicate serials records as suggested by CONSER participants. It is anticipated that in the month of February 1980 alone PRLC will cancel its holding symbol on 250 records. Now with approximately 50,000 PRLC and Pitt local data records and 150,000 holdings on-line, PRLC is in a most advantageous position to concentrate on developing its statewide Pennsylvania union list.

FUTURE ACTIVITIES DURING YEAR ONE

By the end of the second quarter of the contract year, it is expected that the initial system design will be finalized. At the same time, the core group of titles and initial participating libraries will have been identified. Acceptance of the universe of titles and the selected libraries will be sought at the April meeting of the Advisory Committee. Participation of the selected libraries will be sought, and the list of titles will be distributed to the libraries. Using a reporting format designed with ease of on-line data entry in mind, the libraries will report their holdings during the third quarter.

On-line entry of the holdings for the core group of titles will be accomplished during the fourth quarter. In the same quarter, a proposal will be completed for second year funding. Throughout the year, union listing developments at OCLC will be closely followed. The possibility of considering substantial decentralization of holdings input can only be considered when the union listing capability is fully available. Therefore, the extent to which OCLC remains on schedule will have a direct bearing on the near future development of the Pennsylvania Union List of Serials.

LATER CONSIDERATIONS AND PLANS

As was stated previously, some consideration will be given to decentralization of entry holdings data. This would tend to increase the ability of the Pennsylvania Union List of Serials to be maintained when state funding ceases. In addition, the creation of individual local data records for each institutional location will increase the possibility of libraries deciding to use the system for check-in. However, it is probable that continued centralization of bibliographic activities will be recommended. This is a crucial step in quality control and in assuring adherence to national bibliographic standards.

Decisions will need to be made regarding the priorities in the future expansion of the list both in titles and libraries. It seems probable at this stage that similar techniques for expansion of both titles and libraries will be recommended for the second year. However, the need for frequently borrowed titles and for rare titles must be kept in mind. Both types of utilization of a statewide Pennsylvania list must be provided for in planning its development.

An important part of the project is the provision for production of the list in COM. Planning for this will be completed during the second year. Production of a COM list will probably take place during the third year. It will be important to maintain awareness of and cooperation with other similar on-line union list agencies. There may be a demand for COM output by several union list constituencies, and this is a prime area for a cooperative application.

CONCLUSION

Union lists are a traditionally valuable reference source in libraries. Advances in technology enabling on-line union lists have added to this value through increased currency of information plus widespread distribution. The Pennsylvania Union List of Serials when it is available on-line and in COM will be a major service to users of serial resources in state and nationally. In addition, it is hoped that the Pennsylvania Union List will be compatible with other state and regional union lists. Many libraries in West Virginia, for example, are included in the PRLC list. The prospects for large-scale regional lists are both real and exciting.

Future progress in the development of the Pennsylvania Union List of Serials will be reported on a timely basis in order to keep the library community informed on this important project. It is one more effort in the building of a national serials data base and is in accordance with plans for a national serials data system.

REFERENCES

1. Alexander Strasser, *Bibliographic Access in Pennsylvania* (Pittsburgh: Pittsburgh Regional Library Center, 1979).
2. Ruth C. Carter, "Steps toward an On-Line Union List," *Journal of Library Automation* 11, no. 1 (March 1978): 32-40.
3. Carter, "Steps toward," p. 32-40.

The Pennsylvania Union List of Serials: Continuing Development

Ruth C. Carter, MA, MS
Scott Bruntjen, MA, MA, DA

SUMMARY. In 1979 the State Library of Pennsylvania awarded a contract of $99,304 to the Pittsburgh Regional Library Center to begin development of an on-line union list of serials for Pennsylvania. This article describes accomplishments of the first contract year, October 1, 1979-September 30, 1980; the second year proposal for which a contract was awarded for $99,848; and accomplishments to date in the second year of the Pennsylvania Union List of Serials (PaULS). Plans for production of the initial core list of 2,580 titles in COM by June 30, 1981 are described. OCLC developments including the introduction of its union listing capability are discussed and implications of these for the long-range future of PaULS are considered. Planning for the third year and beyond is reviewed and possible applications against the file and its usefulness as a tool for regional collection development are presented.

I. INTRODUCTION

In 1979 the State Library of Pennsylvania awarded the Pittsburgh Regional Library Center (PRLC) a contract for $99,304.44 to begin development of a statewide on-line union list of serials. During year one, October 1, 1979-September 30, 1980, the goals for the Pennsylvania Union List of Serials (PaULS) were to: design a system within the constraints of the OCLC Serials Control sub-system, de-

---

Dr. Bruntjen, MA, MA, DA, is Executive Director, Pittsburgh Regional Library Center, Beatty Hall, Chatham College, Pittsburgh, PA 15232 and Project Administrator, Pennsylvania Union List of Serials, Pittsburgh Regional Library Center, Pittsburgh, PA 15232.

Reprinted from *The Serials Librarian*, Vol. 6(2/3), Winter 1981/Spring 1982.

velop an initial core list of approximately 2,000 titles, and select about fifty libraries to be distributed geographically and by size and type throughout the state. The State Library of Pennsylvania specified that the union list was to be designed with the capability of being produced in COM and the whole effort was to work toward achieving a greater balance between lenders and borrowers of journal interlibrary loans within Pennsylvania.

The historical background and initial system design of PaULS has already been described by Carter and Bruntjen.[1] The present article describes actual accomplishments of year one, the proposal for year two, accomplishments to date in year two, anticipated problem areas, and plans for continued development and maintenance of PaULS.

II. YEAR ONE ACCOMPLISHMENTS

Year one for the Pennsylvania Union List, October 1, 1979-September 30, 1980, went remarkably well. Actual accomplishments generally exceeded original goals. Much of this is attributable to the highly structured approach taken in the initial development of PaULS.

When the State Library of Pennsylvania issued its Request for Proposal, a meeting was called of the PRLC Union List Committee. There was unanimous agreement of the Committee members and the PRLC staff that any proposal submitted should have specific, well-defined goals that were indeed capable of being accomplished in a first year's effort. With the idea of having a goal that was practicable in nature, it was agreed that a "core list" of titles should be developed and that initial participating libraries should be limited in number.

The proposal submitted by PRLC called for the development of a core list of approximately 2,000 titles and 25-35 initial participating libraries. At the end of the first year, both totals were exceeded by at least 25%. The actual core list of titles reached 2,580. Fifty libraries outside of PRLC were invited to be participants. Of these, forty-two returned the data collection form in time to have holdings input as part of the first year project.

Twenty-one libraries in the western part of the state were de facto participants in the new Pennsylvania union list through participation in the PRLC union list. As newly selected libraries were all outside the Pittsburgh Regional Library Center area, a balance was provided within Pennsylvania geographically as well as by size and type of library. Altogether, there were 14 state colleges, 26 district library centers (public libraries), and 39 other academic institutions. The public library district centers were included specifically in order to make their holdings known in the expectation that this would encourage requests to go to them for interlibrary loans.

To assist in the development of a core list of titles 766 libraries in Pennsylvania were surveyed. The questionnaire asked each library to name the five journal titles it had lent most often in the last two years, the five it had requested most often on interlibrary loan in the last two years, and the other titles which it would like to see included in the union list. Two hundred and sixty-four libraries responded. Those that did not respond were almost exclusively school libraries. Therefore, the respondents provided a good return for public, special, and academic libraries.

The questionnaire responses clearly indicated a demand for two types of journals: the very popular titles such as *Science* and *Newsweek*, or the specialized technical journals. For the initial core list, it was decided to emphasize the commonly held and requested titles. Although the purpose of this article is not to go into detail on how individual titles were selected, it seems appropriate to state the general guidelines.

A title selected for the core had to meet at least one of the following criteria. In most cases it met more than one:

1. it appeared in *Reader's Guide*;
2. it appeared in other widely available indexes;
3. it was listed on the questionnaire returns;
4. it was on the list of frequently requested titles in the Science and Technology Library of the Carnegie Library of Pittsburgh;
5. it was on the Library of Congress "List of Commonly Used Periodicals";
6. it was on the list of medical titles not lent by medical libraries;
7. it was an earlier or later title to another core title. (Note: earlier

titles were in general included only if the title change occurred after 1950); or
8. it was a Pennsylvania imprint.

Once the core list was selected, it was typed onto a data collection form (see Figure 1). The form was designed to facilitate large scale entry of holding data. When the lists were returned, they were batched by page in groups of 9 to 13 and alphabetized by OCLC code within each batch. Four passes of the 186 pages of the core were made between July and September 1980. It is estimated that more than 50,000 holdings were entered during this period. The only major problem encountered with the data collection form was that when it was distributed to participants to fill out, it did not include the volumes and dates covered by each title. This resulted in some libraries reporting all holdings under the latest title instead of being recorded for each separate title in accordance with the successive entry records selected for the PaULS list.

III. YEAR TWO PROPOSAL

PRLC submitted its proposal for a second year of development of the Pennsylvania Union List of Serials on June 27, 1980. The proposal was developed with input from the State Library of Pennsylvania, the PaULS Advisory Committee, PaULS staff, the PRLC Executive Committee, and the PRLC Union List Committee. In July 1980, PRLC received notification that it was awarded funding for Year Two of $99,848.

As in year one, the year two proposal specified that all work should be in accordance with national standards and plans. Conformance to national standards has been, from the beginning, a basic commitment for PaULS. The inclusion on the PaULS Advisory Committee of a representative from the Library of Congress and a representative from OCLC have worked to ensure adherence to national standards.

The PaULS staff for year two had one major change. The Coordinator/Editor left, and was replaced by a second Serial Cataloger. The rest of the fulltime staff remained constant: Serial Cataloger, Searcher/Inputter, and Clerk Typist/Terminal Operator. In addition,

PENNSYLVANIA UNION LIST OF SERIALS -- CORE LIST OF TITLES

LIBRARY NAME _____   LIBRARY OCLC CODE _____   REPORT DATE (YEAR/MONTH) _____

TITLE OF MAIN ENTRY/TITLE	OCLC #	VOLUMES HELD	DATE OF COVERAGE	LOCAL NOTES	NON-RE-TENTION CODE
CANADIAN JOURNAL OF ECONOMICS AND POLITICAL SCIENCE	833682				
THE CANADIAN JOURNAL OF HISTORY	1553144				
CANADIAN JOURNAL OF POLITICAL SCIENCE	1553156				
CANADIAN JOURNAL OF PSYCHOLOGY REVUE. CANADIENNE DE PSYCHOLOGIE)	1553157				
CANADIAN JOURNAL OF PUBLIC HEALTH	1553158				
CANADIAN LITERATURE	1553179				
CANADIAN MEDICAL ASSOCIATION JOURNAL	1553185				
CANADIAN NURSE	1553202				
CANCER	1553275				
CANCER RESEARCH (BALTIMORE)	1553285				
CANCER TREATMENT REPORTS	2101497				
CAR AND DRIVER	4814147				
CARIBBEAN STUDIES	844091				
CARNEGIE MAGAZINE	5453926				

FIGURE 1

the PRLC Executive Director is the Project Administrator and the Head of Serials at the University of Pittsburgh is the Technical Director. The project has approximately 25 hours per week of part-time help.

The key goals for the second year of PaULS were: expansion of both titles and libraries, testing of decentralized input, and production of at least the initial core list of serials in COM. Activities related to these goals are described below.

Expansion of titles and libraries. It was agreed to achieve the expansion of titles and libraries in two primary ways. The structured approach to building the file was to continue in the creation of a second controlled list. This was to be the titles in the most recent edition of the union list of serials held by the libraries of the state correctional and mental health institutions. It is planned to identify the correct bibliographic record on OCLC, and then recollect holdings using a prearranged data collection form. In addition, these state institutions will report any titles new to their collections since the compilation of their most recent union list.

The second approach to expansion of the file was to be the reporting of all serial holdings by the special libraries in the PRLC area. Many of these libraries helped found the area union list, and want to continue to participate in its various evolutions. Because, by nature, each special library has a specialized collection, there should be large portions of the collection which are unique or rarely held by others.

Two lesser areas for expansion of the file are the microform titles for titles in the original core list and additional Pennsylvania imprints not previously included. The latter were compiled by Striediecker and Hepler.[2] At the same time as the concerted effort is being made to collect data for the state institutions and some special libraries, most PRLC libraries including the University of Pittsburgh are maintaining their complete union lists on-line on a current basis.

It was acknowledged at the time the proposal was developed that the second year might end up less evenly balanced than the first. However, it was consciously decided to place emphasis during year two on adding holdings for libraries without OCLC. This was because of the availability during the second year of OCLC's union listing capability. Thus, during the third and future years, libraries with OCLC will have the capability of inputting their holdings directly.

Testing of decentralized input. Beginning in January 1981 the Tri-State College Library Consortia (TCLC), which is headquartered at Rosemont College in eastern Pennsylvania, began inputting holdings for its twenty-four libraries for the original core list of titles. TCLC was supplied copies of the data collection form for the core, and has distributed it to its members. The completed core is returned directly to TCLC headquarters. PaULS staff provided TCLC staff with input training in September 1980, and is available for consultation at any time. The PaULS staff will periodically monitor data input and, in addition, it has backed up the on-line file by copying local data and bibliographic records for the core titles from the on-line file. This is feasible because all holdings except those for Pitt are input in one local data record per title. However, OCLC's union listing capability will force a conversion of these records to the new format by the end of 1981. This will be discussed later in the paper.

IV. COM PRODUCTION

Identified in the previous section as a major goal, COM production is one of the most important and difficult tasks of the second year. The initial RFP by the State Library included the requirement that the on-line union list have the capability of production in COM. It stated that this activity was not to take place during the first year but that the file should be designed with that capability.

In the long term the best answer for COM production is to get a tape product from OCLC that can be delivered to a COM vendor, or even to receive COM products directly from OCLC. However, OCLC does not have available at present a tape product that combines bibliographic and local data records. Such a product is not likely to be available in less than two years.

Despite the lack of a tape from OCLC which would lend itself to production of PaULS in COM, specifically microfiche, it was decided that it would be beneficial to library users within Pennsylvania to do at least the core in COM in the second year. Therefore, an alternative method to use of a tape from OCLC had to be devised. This article is written prior to actual accomplishment of the PaULS core titles in COM, and some changes in our plans described below may need to be made in order to accomplish this goal.

Because the PaULS core list of 2,580 titles is a defined, limited number of titles controlled by OCLC number, an interim method to achieve COM was developed. It was also important that only two local data records needed to be accessed to provide the holdings for each PaULS title.

It was decided that COM could be accomplished by the following steps: (1) acquiring a magnetic tape terminal which reads and writes cassettes, and is connected to OCLC by the printer port, (2) copying the bibliographic and local data records from the CRT screen to cassette using the print command, (3) transferring the PaULS data on cassettes to a reel-to-reel tape—perhaps via a microcomputer, (4) turning the reel-to-reel tape into a COM production format, and (5) production of the COM. The steps identified as having the most potential risk of complications were: turning the data on cassette into a reel-to-reel tape and turning the reel-to-reel tape into a COM-ready format.

At the date of the writing of this article (January 1981) investigation is proceeding on the major problem of getting from a cassette to a reel-to-reel tape and getting that tape into a format suitable for COM. Because vendors have had experience using MARC formats, it seems desirable to produce a vendor-ready tape in a MARC-like format.

It is anticipated that the core list of 2,580 titles with holdings for 70 libraries will take between 6 and 9 microfiche. Three thousand copies of the fiche will be produced and distributed to libraries around the state. The State Library expects to provide microfiche readers for many libraries, primarily those with OCLC. Production of PaULS in COM will then provide more users around the state with access to this important finding and decision-making tool. It will be a helpful back-up to the on-line file as well.

V. PROBLEM AREAS

Next to COM production, the area of most concern during the second year of PaULS is the introduction of new charges by OCLC for use of the Serials Control System and Union Listing. The latter includes both an annual union list membership fee and a charge for searching any union list including the list(s) in which an individual institution participates.

Fortunately, the union listing fee will not apply to the Pennsylvania list until the local data records are converted to the union listing format. This is scheduled to take place during the fourth quarter of 1981. One possible advantage to the annual fee is that it does force a commitment on the part of individual libraries and union list agents to active maintenance and use of the union list. This means that any particular union list cannot be taken for granted.

Throughout the second year, PaULS staff must work closely with OCLC to plan for the conversion of the PRLC/PaULS and Pitt local data records to the union listing format. At present there is one local data record per title for PaULS and one for Pitt. After the conversion there will be one local data record for each copy at each library of a title. In the future, OCLC will have a charge on the creation of each local data record. This must be considered in planning for future decentralization of PaULS for holdings maintenance as well as in provision for a central facility inputting data for union list members which are non-OCLC participants.

Other areas of concern during the second year are: getting full participation, especially from the special libraries, and making librarians accustomed to using the on-line union list. It is recognized that more publicity to acquaint public service personnel with the on-line file is needed. In addition, the on-line union list is a powerful tool for use by collection development librarians.

VI. YEAR THREE

As of the date of this writing it appears probable that there will be at least a year three. However, it is expected that it will be funded at less than the $100,000.00 level. Reduced funding combined with the conversion of PaULS records to the union listing format will mean that year three is probably the critical year for the long range maintenance of PaULS. It will be important to develop procedures and provide training for decentralization of some functions, particularly the holdings input by participants who have OCLC. It is expected that bibliographic activities will continue to be coordinated centrally. This is necessary to provide high quality in input of new records as well as consistency in choice of bibliographic records.

The production of a second COM union list is another probable feature of a third year's activities. Emphasis for COM II may be titles held by the state institutions. Although it is not possible at this date to describe precisely the features of year three, it is certainly not too early to be giving serious consideration to the best ways of continuing to develop and maintain PaULS. The proposal will be submitted in May and actual funding should be announced in June or July, 1981.

VII. FUTURE APPLICATIONS AND OTHER POSSIBLE PaULS DEVELOPMENTS

During the second year, titles and libraries are being added to PaULS unevenly. Special libraries in the west are adding all their titles, state institutions are adding all their titles, and the TCLC libraries in eastern Pennsylvania are adding the core list of titles. PaULS is also expanding through input of all changes and additions to the University of Pittsburgh union list and the comprehensive reporting by many PRLC libraries. It is expected that during the third and future years OCLC libraries throughout the state may input their holdings directly.

If possible, it would be advantageous to get several large union lists or libraries with substantial holdings to do retrospective conversions. Costs will undoubtedly be a factor in how much, if any, of this can be accomplished. At a minimum, it is hoped that there will be a commitment to file building and maintenance from this point forward.

Work to date has created a substantial data base in PaULS. Its most obvious use is as a finding tool, but PaULS lends itself to other applications, particularly in the area of regional collection development. One early application may be a method of communicating cancellation decisions. The need for this is substantial, as cancellation decisions are often made simultaneously due to budgetary and subscription cycles. Holdings cannot be closed until the last issue of a subscription is received. Often this does not occur until a year or more after the cancellation order is placed. In order to preserve the last copy in a region or in the state, a method should be developed to systematic communicating of the cancellation decision. The on-line union list seems a natural mechanism to convey the information. Development of a standard method to accomplish this communication is presently under consideration.

VIII. CONCLUSION

To date, PaULS has proven to have a sound design, and established goals have been met. During the first two years funding has been adequate to make significant advances in the task of initial file construction. During the third year, PaULS must adapt to changes in its union list which are mandated by OCLC's introduction of the union listing capability.

Assuming the provision of adequate funding for the third year and the crucial shift from development to a maintenance mode, PaULS should be in a position to fulfill its initial goals of leveling the borrowing and lending levels of journal materials within Pennsylvania and in making the serial resources of Pennsylvania better known and more widely available. Furthermore, it has the capability of serving as a regional link in an emerging national periodical system and as a data base which offers the opportunity for managing regional collection development in order that greatest number of resources can be in the state and general area.

The development of PaULS during the next two years will be a considerable challenge due to change, some funding uncertainties, and establishing the tradition of an on-line union list of serials. However, in the long term, various obstacles and complications should have been resolved, and Pennsylvania will be in an advantageous position to meet the demands for serials resources by its library community during the 1980s and beyond.

REFERENCES

1. Carter, Ruth C. and Scott Bruntjen, "The Pennsylvania Union List of Serials: Initial Development," *The Serials Librarian*, 5:3 Spring 1981.
2. Striediecker, Suzanne and William Hepfer, "Pennsylvania's Periodicals," *Serials Review*: 43-52, April/June 1980.

The Pennsylvania Union List of Serials: From Development to Maintenance

Ruth C. Carter, MA, MS
Scott Bruntjen, MA, MA, DA

SUMMARY. The Pennsylvania Union List of Serials (PaULS) is presently in the process of transition from development to maintenance. Since October 1, 1979, its development has been supported by the State Library of Pennsylvania with LSCA funds. The current article describes accomplishments of PaULS from early 1981 through April 1983 including the production of its "core titles" in COM fiche and the conversion of its records by OCLC to the format required for the union listing capability. Current and future problems for PaULS are discussed as are long-term maintenance issues. In addition, PaULS' role as one part of the national serials database is examined.

INTRODUCTION

The Pennsylvania Union List of Serials (PaULS) is online with OCLC. It has at least 60,000 titles and several hundred thousand holdings. Holdings represent approximately 250 participating libraries primarily in Pennsylvania and West Virginia. A few additional participants are in Maryland, New Jersey, and Delaware.

As this paper is written (April 1983) the Pennsylvania Union List of Serials is in its fourth year of funding with Library Services and Construction Act (LSCA) Title III (Interlibrary Cooperation) monies from the State Library of Pennsylvania. The first three years were essentially all development. The early development steps have been described previously by Carter and Bruntjen.[1,2] The fourth and current year represents a transition from development to maintenance.

The development stage was characterized by substantial amounts of central funding, central input of data by a central staff, central coordination, physically merged records, and central coordination. The development stage was the easy stage. This is not to imply that the first three years of PaULS were without difficulty, for that was not the case. However, in comparison to maintenance, the tasks involved in development were more straightforward and readily monitored.

The transition to maintenance means a number of basic shifts for PaULS. Funding for PaULS is and will continue to be increasingly distributed; there is less central input and the records for each participant are not physically separated; central coordination exists but much of the detail is shifting to the two networks (the Pittsburgh Regional Library Center [PRLC] and PALINET). Maintaining the Pennsylvania Union List of Serials is in many ways more difficult than getting it started.

This paper will briefly update the development of PaULS from the middle of the second year to the present. It will focus on the transition to maintenance and will examine the key issues in the long-term maintenance of PaULS. These issues include: organization and governance, coordination, quality control, staffing, monitoring the quantity and quality of work, and funding. The article will also summarize problems to date and possible future problems.

PaULS-2

During the second year of development of the Pennsylvania Union List of Serials, the List expanded in three ways. First, holdings for additional libraries beyond the 42 first year participants were added for the initial "core" list of 2,580 titles. Some of these holdings were added in a decentralized site test conducted by the Tri State College Library Consortium (TCLC). Second, an additional "core" or structured list was developed for titles in the union list of serials previously compiled for the state institutions (mental health and correctional facilities in Pennsylvania). Third, special libraries in western Pennsylvania were asked to report their serial holdings on a comprehensive basis. Approximately 20 libraries responded. Many of those libraries had been in the last printed edition of the

Pittsburgh Regional Library Center Union List of Periodicals, which was published in 1973.

The other major area of activity during the second year revolved around plans to produce the first core list of 2,580 titles in COM fiche. As previously described by Carter and Bruntjen[3] the original plan was to copy the data from the bibliographic and local data records from the terminal display to a magnetic tape cassette. That plan gave way to improved technology and the records were copied onto floppy disks via a microcomputer. Programming was then developed to convert the display screen images into MARC-like records in order that they could be processed by a vendor. Although this process began during PaULS-2 and was originally scheduled for completion during that contract year, the actual accomplishment of the COM production did not occur until late in the PaULS-3 contract year. However, as of this writing, the PaULS COM fiche remains the only widely distributed product combining OCLC bibliographic and local data records. Obviously, the method used to accomplish its production is labor intensive, error prone, and slow and would not be feasible for larger, unstructured files. Despite problems and delays, however, it is a significant accomplishment because the core titles and holdings for approximately 100 libraries of the titles most frequently requested on interlibrary loan have now been distributed to almost 2,000 libraries throughout Pennsylvania and West Virginia. Most of the libraries reached via the COM do not and probably will not have direct access to an OCLC terminal.

PaULS-3

The third year of PaULS, October 1, 1981 to September 30, 1982, was supported with LSCA funds of $91,000. Major activities of PaULS-3 included addition of holdings for selected special libraries in eastern Pennsylvania, the addition of more libraries to the years 1 and 2 core lists, and the continuation of cataloging and holdings entry generated in the second year. In addition, there was considerable work with OCLC on specifications and plans for the conversion of the Pennsylvania Union List of Serials records including those of the University of Pittsburgh to the format required by OCLC's union listing capability.

During PaULS-3 the COM microfiche of the 2,580 core titles was completed. It was distributed to approximately 2,000 libraries in Pennsylvania and other selected libraries. This finding aid has been well received. Because the titles on the core list are the most frequently requested on interlibrary loan, possession of this access tool is useful to libraries of all sizes and types. The process of producing the list brought home the fact that there is no agreed upon standard for communicating holdings and locations. It is hoped that work in process on the MARC Format for Holdings and Locations will soon be approved so that communication of holdings data can be standardized.

One of the major activities of PaULS-3 was the education and training provided Pennsylvania librarians in the use and maintenance of PaULS. The primary vehicle for this effort was a series of five workshops conducted in different regions of Pennsylvania in May and June of 1982. Because of the number of West Virginia participants, PRLC provided a sixth workshop so that librarians for those institutions could benefit from the effort as well. The workshop consisted of instruction in putting data to PaULS in the new union listing format. It also provided guidance in searching online union lists and record selection. The workshops were held in the latter part of the PaULS-3 contract year in order to put them as close as possible to the conversion of PaULS data to the union listing format. This will be described in more detail later, but the conversion was important in enabling the change from a highly centralized operation to one that is largely decentralized.

PaULS-4

By May 1982 it became apparent that the PaULS record conversion would not take place during PaULS-3 or, if it did, it would be too late to deal with the problems that it would generate. Recognizing the need to deal with the technical issues of the conversion as well as to provide some coordination when the Pennsylvania Union List of Serials became decentralized, the State Library of Pennsylvania provided LSCA funding of approximately $60,000 for a fourth year of development. The fourth and present year at the time of the writing of this article was also seen as a year of transition and planning for the long-term future of PaULS. In addition, it was hoped that offline products for union listing would become available from OCLC. Funds were carried over from PaULS-3 to support a second PaULS fiche.

The actual conversion of the PaULS records took place over two weekends in November 1982. It was done in two parts because the University of Pittsburgh local data records were processed as one group, and the PRLC/PaULS local data records were converted as a separate file. Prior to the conversion there was a maximum of two local data records for any title in PaULS—one record for Pitt and one record for PRCL/PaULS. Thus, if fifty PaULS participants held the same title, the holdings for all fifty were entered in one local data record. Obviously, this encouraged centralization of input. The conversion created a separate local data record for each copy of each title for each participating library. The physical separation into individual records now encourages decentralized input and maintenance of the records.

The actual conversion when it happened went fairly smoothly. Most errors encountered were input or profiling errors, although there were some problems with local data records for libraries that were using the check-in function. Libraries in PaULS were asked to check their records after the conversion. The most serious problem appears to be one of omission. Some libraries found that about 10% of the titles that they thought had holdings online did not. At this point in the process, it is difficult to determine the source of the problem. Fortunately, most libraries have expressed a commitment to keeping the data up to date and are, therefore, creating the necessary records. It is clear that the conversion to the union listing format is a key factor in making the long-term maintenance of PaULS possible.

A number of major issues have been identified that must be resolved during the transition phase. They include:

> How should PaULS be organized?
> How should PaULS be governed?
> Who should coordinate PaULS? This year? Next year and beyond?
> What should be the relationship of small union list groups to PaULS as a whole?
> How can quality control be achieved?

How can file activity be monitored to ensure participation?
What offline products are required? By whom? How will they be paid for?
Who will pay for PaULS? When? How much?
How will provision be made for updating or adding holdings for non-OCLC libraries?

USER REACTIONS

The PaULS-3 contract called for a user survey. However, with a change in format imminent, it was decided to wait until after the conversion. As of the writing of this article, a formal survey has not yet been conducted. However, there is a growing body of feedback on the value and satisfaction of PaULS. Part of this was generated with the distribution of the COM fiche. The large majority of comments received to date have praised the value of PaULS as distributed on the COM fiche, even with the limitation of the fiche to the "core" titles. Because these titles are the most frequently requested on interlibrary loan, the widespread availability of holdings for these titles has provided a significant service to the users of PaULS. A number of libraries that received the PaULS fiche but were not participants have requested to be included in PaULS because they would like to reciprocate the benefits gained. This, of course, raises the issue of how to pay for entry of data for non-OCLC libraries. That topic will be discussed further on in this paper.

Libraries with a large proportion of their serial titles online with OCLC appear to be receiving a large number of blind interlibrary loan requests, i.e., the institution's symbol appears on OCLC but the institution does not hold the volume in question. This would appear to mean that requesting libraries are not searching for serial holdings via union listing. Therefore, it is apparent that more user education is required. If the interlibrary loan initiator checks holdings through union list commands as opposed to merely checking holdings in cataloging, the requesting library can ascertain whether or not the holding library has the specific volume in question as opposed to just having some piece of the total run of an item. Perhaps the introduction of a charge for the "dh" (display holdings) command in July 1983 will encourage interlibrary loan users to search for serial holdings with the union list display commands, as there will be no charge at this time for the latter.

There is a strong potential to expand the use of union list data to collection development/management issues. This area was tested during 1981/1982 in a grant awarded to the Pittsburgh Regional Library Center by the Council on Library Resources. The grant was for the purpose of communicating decisions to cancel serial subscriptions in a widespread fashion at the time the cancellation decisions are made. The idea for the grant proposal came from events in western Pennsylvania in the spring of 1980. During the Spring and Summer of 1980, many libraries in western Pennsylvania, including but not limited to most academic libraries, had to make significant cuts in their serial subscriptions. Because the budget year and subscriptions cycles tended to be the same, decisions had to be made more or less simultaneously at a number of different institutions.

The authors of this paper were involved with institutions and the region generally affected by the subscriptions cut. Because they were in the process of working with the development of the Pennsylvania Union List of Serials, they recognized that PaULS was an ideal medium to communicate the cancellation decisions. Therefore, they proposed and received funding to develop a prototype pilot project to enter cancellation decisions online at the time they were made and to conduct workshops throughout Pennsylvania and West Virginia for the purpose of enhancing awareness among collection development librarians and library managers of the capability of the online union lists for communicating this information. In general, it was considered that moving to an applications phase following the period in which large bibliographic and holdings files were constructed was particularly appropriate. Online large-scale union lists represent a very useful tool for collection management. Their potential is only beginning to be explored. The Serial Cancellation Pilot Project was completed in early 1983. The concept of utilizing widespread online services to communicate serial cancellation data, preferably in a standardized manner, was substantiated as worthwhile. This project will be described separately in appropriate library literature.

PROBLEMS DURING THE DEVELOPMENT OF PaULS

As was stated previously, in many ways the period of development and large-scale file building on what amounts to a project basis is easier than prospective file maintenance. Actual problems encountered in the development phase of PaULS have been minimal. Nevertheless, a few are readily identifiable. These problems are listed below:

1. Completion of the conversion by OCLC of the PaULS Local Data Records to the format required for the union listing capability. Although the actual conversion went as well as could be expected, it was rescheduled many times, and was carried out approximately one year later than originally expected. This necessitated a largely centralized operation for longer than anticipated. In addition, the workshops to provide training for decentralized input were conducted up to six months prior to the conversion rather than shortly afterward. This meant that there were more questions on updating and also that the enthusiasm generated by the workshops was less apparent by the time the conversion was accomplished and individual libraries could begin to maintain their own data.

2. Accomplishing the production of the COM fiche was also a problem area. It was, if anything, even more labor intensive than first anticipated. Second, the process was generally more complicated and error-prone than expected. Third, there were delays or problems at almost every step. However, this did result in a unique product and one that has proved very useful. The slippage in the actual production of the COM fiche from PaULS-2 to PaULS-3 meant that monies had to be carried over from one contract year to another; and while that was not a significant problem, it was one minor extra detail to be accounted for.

3. Some libraries did not report as had been expected. This group includes one District Library Center and several of the state institutions. Furthermore, not as many special libraries contributed data as had been hoped. There were no more than a total of thirty special libraries.

4. The bibliographic work exceeds the capacity of PaULS bibliographic staff. In general, it seems that the cataloging keeps mush-

rooming, and that this is in part due to the nature of serials cataloging, which is very complicated. From the outset all bibliographic work on PaULS has followed national standards, including successive entry records and separate records for each format of the same title. This has required the creation of a great many new records. The introduction of AACR2 has further complicated matters because a hardcopy record already in the database might be cataloged in accordance with pre-AACR2 rules and a microform record being entered would need to be cataloged in accordance with AACR2. The bibliographic work is less dramatic in terms of quantity than holdings work; however, it is necessary and important in two significant ways. On the one hand, those records receiving cataloging by PaULS staff are for titles not in the OCLC database or, if they are in and are incomplete, are rarely held. Cataloging these titles then is a substantial contribution to the national serials database. Second, the holdings for any particular title cannot be entered unless a bibliographic record is present. Thus, cataloging is essential if comprehensive inclusion of the participating libraries' holdings are to be accomplished. Naturally, PaULS cataloging has complimented and supplemented cataloging by many of its participants and is not the only source of cataloging for the unique titles held by PaULS libraries. One area in which the PaULS' contribution to bibliographic control has been most evident is in titles held by participating special libraries.

5. Staff turnover, although not excessive, has tended to happen at critical junctures. During the first year of PaULS the full-time professional staff consisted of one Coordinator/Editor, one Serials Cataloger, and one Searcher/Inputter. These were assisted by several part-time inputters as well as the Technical Director and Project Administrator. During the second year of PaULS, the position of Coordinator/Editor was replaced by a second Serials Cataloger (The Searcher/Inputter from PaULS-1). A new Searcher/Inputter was hired, and that position evolved into the position of Holdings Editor. At the end of PaULS-2, it was necessary to replace the original Serials Cataloger. The second Serials Cataloger position was not funded after PaULS-3.

Probably the most serious staff change came early in PaULS-4 when the Holding Editor resigned. This position was filled for most of the remainder of PaULS-4, but it was a difficult time to make the change, particularly in light of the need to resolve errors produced during the conversion process. In addition, as would be expected, there have been a number of turnovers in part-time inputters. This has presented a more-or-less continuous training problem. Fortunately, two part-time inputters with a high degree of skill have been with the project since its inception.

CURRENT AND FUTURE PROBLEMS

Surprisingly enough, a nagging problem has been in trying to determine who belongs to the Pennsylvania Union List of Serials. Just the issue of who belongs has brought more difficulties than expected. One reason is that it turns out that there are two "profiles" for union listing at OCLC. The profile that is best known is the profile specifying which members of a union list should be displayed together. An equally important profile, especially if a responsible body does not realize that there are two, is the "profile" that indicates for which libraries the union list agent is authorized to enter updates. Errors in profiling either by the union list agent or by OCLC will show up readily if either category of profile is not consistent. This happened in PaULS' maintenance when the "ulpasu" command would display a particular library's holdings, but the command "ldrxxx" would not retrieve the local data record for update purposes. In any event, these are two profiles which need to be kept up-to-date with OCLC. As in any other area involving paperwork, it takes a separate, conscientious effort to make sure that all records match. This includes those of individual participant, the union list agent(s), and OCLC.

A major issue both in the short term and probably in the long term, is trying to get the individual participating libraries to update their own records. To some extent this seems to be more of a problem in eastern Pennsylvania than in western Pennsylvania or West Virginia. Perhaps, it is because the latter two areas have had traditions of large-scale union lists of serials, and consequently are more amenable to one more update, if necessary. If must be noted, however, that ideally the time will come when one update will serve all purposes and multiple update of the same data will not be necessary.

One of the reasons why it is difficult to convince individual libraries to actually update data online is that this is against conventional patterns of providing union listing data. Many manual union lists have been customarily updated on a special project basis. For example, when it was time to produce a new union list each library would be notified, and the libraries would then update their records. This is a possible, but undesirable, approach with an online union list. Online union lists get their maximum effectiveness when the data are current. Particularly important examples of this are the creation of a holdings record(s), when the first issue of a title is received and the entry of the decision to cancel a serial subscription. The only way to solve the problem in a continuingly satisfactory way is for all OCLC participants of a union list of serials to build the maintenance routines into ongoing check-in and subscription routines. Anything short of incorporating online union list maintenance as part of continuing procedures will fall short of the capabilities of having all this massive data online.

Another key issue and potential problem is determining the best method for organizing and the way in which PaULS can be funded for the forseeable future. Funding and organization are closely interrelated issues. One step in the direction of providing for future funding has been the decentralization of input to libraries with OCLC. Because the PaULS OCLC libraries will update directly, the cost of the Local Data Record creation, update and storage will be billed to those libraries. It is unrealistic in any case to expect that the State Library of Pennsylvania with LSCA monies or any other means will continue to subsidize such a large proportion of PaULS costs.

The answers to organizational questions at the time of this writing are even less clear. Several basic alternatives exist as to an organizational/governance structure for PaULS. The two concerns of organization and governance are partly overlapping and partly separate. Issues involved include, among others, the setting of policies and procedures, staffing and training. And many questions need answering: what is the relationship of the two networks? how can funding be raised? who can contract for services? what will be the channels for invoicing? who will prepare grant proposals? what is the relationship with the State Library of Pennsylvania? and so on.

Several basic options exist. They are: (1) Each library (OCLC) can be an independent participant with coordination loosely provided by the networks; (2) The primary responsibility for PaULS can shift directly to the State Library, which would then coordinate training and membership and monitor progress, or; (3) PaULS could be incorporated as a separate entity. Although it is not yet determined what the configuration will be, the latter has several factors in its favor. These are: (1) it would provide consistency in procedures and policies; (2) PaULS could have members from more than one network and because it would be a private corporation, it could involve the various libraries in its activities; (3) it would provide a body either to hire staff, coordinate with OCLC and receive and transmit invoices or to contract for such services; (4) it could have a Board of Directors to enable broad-based direction; and (5) it is a structure that could encompass non-OCLC libraries readily.

As was stated previously, the answer to the future organization for PaULS' activities has not been decided. This will be debated in a PaULS Advisory Committee meeting in May 1983 and in other forums in succeeding months. Although there may be LSCA funding either to the contractor presently developing PaULS (PRLC) or to a separate corporation for the PaULS-5 year beginning October 1, 1983, it is clear that by mid-PaULS-5, the answers to PaULS organizational governance questions must be known.

OCLC ONLINE ACCESS FOR NON-OCLC CATALOGING LIBRARIES

Ever since the initial formation of the original Ohio College Library Center, one of the basic philosophical tenets of the cooperative was that libraries had to add their data to the OCLC online union catalog before they could benefit online from the products and services that were available. This philosophy was enforced through contracts with regional networks that required that any library wishing access to the OCLC database had to do all of its current cataloging on OCLC.

When union listing became available, however, OCLC recognized the possibility that collections important for a regional union list might be in non-OCLC libraries, and for that reason permitted such libraries to have their data entered by an agent. While their data could be seen by OCLC participants in the union list, these libraries could only have access to the union list—and even their own data—through offline products. Nevertheless, this work with non-OCLC libraries through an agent was the first break with the long-time requirement that all current cataloging had to be first done on the system before an institution could benefit from the system's services.

Over the past several years interest in and use of several online databases has been growing. The use of such services as DIALOG, Orbit, and BRS is now well documented, and that work provided many non-OCLC libraries (often smaller corporate libraries) with dial-up equipment and training in database searching. As the OCLC database in dial-up mode is different in the way it is used from any other tool, interest in using it for support of interlibrary loan is growing.

Thus, on the one hand several special libraries in the PaULS list had had their data entered by an agent as they were non-OCLC libraries while, on the other hand, they wanted access to those data and to the larger OCLC database but did not feel they could justify complete cataloging on OCLC. At the same time, OCLC was approaching smaller libraries for online interlibrary loan and had begun to develop a new concept: "Group Access."

Group Access as initially conceived by OCLC was to provide access to the OCLC data base in dial-up mode, and it was limited to the bibliographic record data elements needed for interlibrary loan so as to provide regional online interlibrary loan without the contract requirement for all current cataloging. To test the concept, OCLC wanted a limited number of test sites that would work with the idea during 1983 and 1984.

The use of the Group Access concept by a union list group that included a number of non-OCLC libraries was a natural, for it would provide incentive to those libraries to continue to update their records since they could see them online for the first time and, as important, it did not change the basic OCLC cooperative philosophy of adding data to the system before benefiting from it. In the case of PaULS, most non-OCLC libraries were special libraries that already had the needed dial-up equipment and database searching expertise.

In the Spring of 1983, PRLC was selected as one of four test sites for Group Access, and of this writing has begun to invite the special libraries in the PRLC region to participate in Group Access during 1983 and 1984. If successful, this should both promote the maintenance of those holdings in PaULS, while working toward the initial goal of leveling the lending and borrowing rates among libraries of all types within Pennsylvania.

OFFLINE PRODUCTS

Securing offline products continues to be an issue of major concern. As mentioned previously, there are two major options. One option is to produce another controlled partial list of PaULS holdings via a labor intensive "local" production. The second, and more desirable method, is for OCLC to make offline products available as it has promised. At a minimum this should mean that every union list or individual participant within a union list should be able to order hardcopy printouts or mircofiche for its holdings. In addition, any union list agent should be able to obtain a tape at a reasonable price of the holdings of the entire union list group, and this should contain both bibliographic and holdings data. Offline products from OCLC and ongoing storage of data on OCLC both pose questions in regard to costs. This is a very delicate area and one that requires considerable balance between cost recovery for OCLC and what individual participants are willing to pay. It must be noted that individual libraries are participating on a good faith basis and that part of that good faith basis is that economies of scale will be available to them. In other words, OCLC should be able to store and otherwise maintain union list data for participants and produce needed offline products for them more cheaply than they can do it themselves, whether the "themself" is a single institution or a local, regional, or state group.

CONCLUSIONS

In looking at almost four years of activity on the Pennsylvania Union List of Serials, the first most obvious conclusion to the writers is that PaULS has proceeded amazingly well. Almost everything that it was said would be accomplished has been accomplished on or very close to the specified time. The success to date leads to the expectation that with the continued support and encouragement of the State Library of Pennsylvania PaULS will continue to become more comprehensive and will stay up-to-date. It will therefore become an even more important state, regional, and national resource.

Second, even though the answer to each individual maintenance issue may not be clearly known at present, it is virtually certain that these issues will be resolved satisfactorily. The original reasons for PaULS are still valid. This includes the need for one finding tool for serial resources within the State of Pennsylvania instead of the multiplicity of sources that existed previously.

Furthermore, PaULS is one part of the national serials database. In this regard it is important that the unique or rarely held serial resources within the State become known. The issue has been addressed in separate funding proposals that may or may not receive positive action. Pennsylvania wants to participate in the United States Newspaper Project, and some newspaper holdings are already online with PaULS. This is particularly true with the newspaper holdings of the University of Pittsburgh. In the 1970s, PRLC had a list of newspaper holdings of its members. Updating of this list is being held for incorporation into the Newspaper Project.

As with all automated functions, PaULS and online union listing are in a state of transition. Certainly the potential has been and is being demonstrated daily. Extra projects such as the Serials Cancellation Project funded by the Council on Library Resources illustrate the many capabilities and values of large, online databases. Ideas such as the Group Access capability for Interlibrary Loan and Union Listing participation by non-OCLC libraries have substantial implications for further involvement by many non-cataloging libraries.

If there is a negative in the picture at the present time, other than getting individual participants to correctly maintain their own data on a current basis, it is in the area of prices set by OCLC. Because OCLC is producing union lists products, both online and offline, for multiple groups of libraries and individual institutions, it is expected that these be cost-effective relative to what would be required for an individual participating institution or group if the library or group were doing the work itself. Many libraries and groups, including CONSER and the United States Newspaper Project, have participated through OCLC in good faith. If copyright restrictions for the OCLC database or prices for either online storage and maintenance or offline products become prohibitive, it is certain that alternatives will be found. Individual libraries and institutions have participated in OCLC union listing out of the idea of providing service to users nationwide as a primary goal, not because local alternatives for needed local products are not available. Participants in the Pennsylvania Union List of Serials will continue to proceed in that national cooperative spirit in good faith as long as possible.

REFERENCES

1. Carter, Ruth C. and Scott Bruntjen, "The Pennsylvania Union List of Serials: Initial Development," *The Serials Librarian*, 5:57-64, Spring 1981.
2. Carter, Ruth C. and Scott Bruntjen, "The Pennsylvania Union List of Serials: Continuing Development," *The Serials Librarian*, 6:47-55, Winter 1981/Spring 1982.
3. *Ibid.* p. 52-53.

The Pennsylvania Union List of Serials: Maintenance and Beyond

Ruth C. Carter, MA, MS
James D. Hooks, MLS, PhD

SUMMARY. This article reviews the activities of the Pennsylvania Union List of Serials (PaULS) and updates the status to early 1987. Developments following the end of formal support to PaULS by the State Library of Pennsylvania in late 1984 are described. Efforts to put PaULS on a firm maintenance base are examined. The roles of the State Library of Pennsylvania, the Pittsburgh Regional Library Center (PRLC), Palinet, and individual institutions participating in PaULS are discussed. Some consideration is given to the future of PaULS.

BACKGROUND

Formal development of the Pennsylvania Union List of Serials (PaULS) was initiated in 1979 when the State Library of Pennsylvania (SLP) awarded a Library Services and Construction Act (LSCA) grant of $99,304 to the Pittsburgh Regional Library Center (PRLC) for the purpose of developing a statewide online union list of serials. The SLP specified that the union list must be developed and available through the OCLC system.

PaULS was one of the earliest union lists of serials online with OCLC. It was able to get off to a fast start due to the fact that it used the existing union lists of PRLC and the University of Pittsburgh

---

The authors wish to acknowledge the contributions to this paper of H. E. Broadbent III, Executive Director, Pittsburgh Regional Library Center, and Charles Peguese, Coordinator, Resource Sharing and Academic Libraries, State Library of Pennsylvania.

Reprinted from *The Serials Librarian*, Vol. 13(1), September 1987.

(Pitt) as a base. Both of those entities had their serial holdings online with OCLC. Although the existence of the Pitt and PRLC databases online presented problems such as incomplete data and soon to be obsolete formats, they provided a base on which to build and served as an incentive to bring all online data to full national standards. In addition, considerable holdings information was available to PaULS users at an early stage.

The Pennsylvania Union List of Serials had LSCA support for five years and totaled $381,001. (See Appendix A.) Most of the first year, October 1, 1979–September 30, 1980, was devoted to planning and developing a strategy for building the list incrementally. At the same time, PaULS was designed to provide maximum benefits to a large number of users as early in the process as possible. This led to the strategy of developing a core list of 2500 of the most widely held and in demand titles.

The initial development and implementation of PaULS, including the core list and subsequent steps, has been described in detail by Carter and Bruntjen.[1,2,3] That information will not be repeated in this article. Rather, this article will review the maintenance issues raised in the third article of the serials. "The Pennsylvania Union List of Serials: From Development to Maintenance," describe what has or has not happened to date, look at current and future maintenance, and suggest future directions including possible application using the PaULS database.

The final year of LSCA support for PaULS covered October 1, 1983–September 30, 1984. It was expected that the fifth and presumably last year of financial support from outside the participants would concentrate on identification and resolution of maintenance issues. All those concerned, including the State Library of Pennsylvania, the two networks (PRLC and Palinet), and PaULS participants were charged with development of possible maintenance strategies. Input was also sought from the Advisory Committee which had representatives from the Library of Congress and OCLC, Inc.

There was general concern in 1984 that maintenance would suffer without outside funding. Despite the commitment of some institutions to PaULS and their integration of maintenance into routine serials control procedures, this was characteristic of a minority of the participants.

TRANSITION TO PaULS MAINTENANCE

As the fourth year of PaULS approached in the fall of 1982, the long anticipated problem of local maintenance was becoming reality. Although union list efforts are often called projects, they require constant effort and are never really finished. During the development period, holdings changes for most libraries, with the exception of the University of Pittsburgh, were collected on forms, submitted to PRLC, and entered into the OCLC database centrally.

The transition to a maintenance mode for PaULS carried implications that most participating libraries would be responsible for creating or changing their own local data records with their serial holdings. Since a central site for union list development, established at PRLC headquarters, was expected to terminate at the close of PaULS-4, local sites would have to be established and maintained if participants were to keep the union list viable. Feasibility of local maintenance, training personnel, and promoting local commitment would be essential for the transition.

One group vitally concerned with the problem was the PRLC Serials Management Committee. Its members realized that local union list activity would not be a high priority project for most libraries, and if adopted, it would most likely have to be accomplished with existing staff. A pilot study was needed to provide observable data to support the feasibility of local maintenance. Arrangements were made with Indiana University of Pennsylvania (IUP) to undertake a pilot project which would test the feasibility of both union list maintenance and dial access capabilities.

Dial access was significant because it was becoming more common as a means of OCLC participation. A number of PaULS contributors, including many of the special libraries, had or would have direct access to OCLC in dial access mode only. It was helpful that one of the state university libraries, Indiana University of Pennsylvania, had dial access as the means of OCLC participation at its branch campus and had staff with a strong interest in PaULS. During the nine-month experimentation period (1982-1983), IUP input and reviewed approximately 200 records per month. No major problems were encountered in updating PaULS using existing personnel or by utilizing dial access terminals. The most notable inconvenience was the necessity of rekeying an entire field in order to add or change one or more characters. Union list maintenance, however, was significantly improved following OCLC conversion to the new union list format. The previously utilized RTHD (retrospective holdings) field was discontinued on May 31, 1982 and replaced by the SCHD (summary copy) and SIHD (summary institution) fields. Later in 1982 the union list conversion to the new format was completed by OCLC, and the first PaULS[4] procedural manual was compiled and edited by Timothy Sperry at PRLC.

Having established that local union list maintenance was possible with existing or part-time personnel, the committee focused its attention on the need to provide training both from philosophical and practical perspectives. Library staff performing the actual inputting would need to learn basic procedures in order to format the holdings data properly while library management would need to be aware of issues and concepts of union listing in order to protect the integrity of such a project. In fact, the first efforts in this area were a series of workshops conducted in 1982 as part of the activities of PaULS-3. Those workshops provided discussions and demonstrations on both searching techniques and maintenance. Because this was the first effort toward decentralization on a large scale, considerable attention was given to bibliographic record selection, local data record creation, and quality control.

By the time PaULS-5 was underway, the PRLC Union List Committee was renamed the PRLC Serials Management Committee to better show its broader scope. That committee was aware that the continued success of PaULS rested with its participating institutions. It decided to sponsor a program at the 1984 PRLC Spring Conference. The session consisted of representatives of a special library, a large university library, a technical library collection, and one managed via dial access, describing how union list maintenance procedures could be incorporated into the daily work of a participating institution. Sessions at the 1985 PRLC conference included presentations that combined union listing demonstrations with an informal information booth to provide conference attendees with opportunities to discuss union list issues and ask questions. Similar efforts were undertaken by Palinet staff.

Despite the efforts of the union list committee and the staffs of the two networks, the response has not been substantial. Although the various conference presentations were well received, they have not produced a fruitful or widespread response to union list commitment. The most noteworthy achievement has been an increase in the level of awareness of the existence of PaULS, particularly by interlibrary loan personnel who are its most frequent users. Obtaining copy specific data from a union list database has significantly decreased the number of unfillable interlibrary loan requests and consequently improved the turnaround time for periodical article requests.

CONTRACTED MAINTENANCE ACTIVITIES

Although it is recognized that ideally PaULS should be maintained directly by each participant, in some cases this is not feasible and in others it is not considered desirable even if technically possible.

Non-OCLC libraries including many special libraries are not able to maintain PaULS directly. Consequently, some means needed to be found to provide an updating capability. This involves submitting holdings information to an agent and also paying for that activity. This issue has been debated throughout the PaULS effort. There is concern that non-OCLC libraries won't participate if they have to pay the costs themselves: conversely, there is the belief that all participants should help support it. This is an area where no long-term solution has been reached.

Many of the OCLC libraries that are PaULS participants have limited staffs and do not want to take on ongoing maintenance activity that requires keeping staff trained. Other OCLC PaULS libraries may be willing to do ongoing maintenance but want to have retrospective conversion of their serial holdings done outside the library on a project basis. The result of this type of concern is a contract business for conversion and/or maintenance of union list holdings.

To date PRLC and Palinet are the primary contractors for PaULS conversion and maintenance especially since PaULS has become the union list of choice. The Lehigh Valley Association of Independent Colleges (LVAIC), a consortium of six college libraries, contracted with PRLC in October, 1984 for a union list project. The project was funded by a LSCA Title III Grant awarded by the State Library of Pennsylvania. The Request For Proposal (RFP) and subsequent memoranda established guidelines for record creation, updating, and quality control. The LVAIC union list consisted of approximately 21,000 titles and 36,000 holdings; guidelines specified posting holdings according to exceptional entry. PRLC staff handle all parts of the process—from record selection to entry of holdings.

The Carnegie Museum of Natural History project is also funded with LSCA Title III funds from the State Library of Pennsylvania. Workflow in this project differs from the LVAIC project in that the Museum staff locates the best union list bibliographic record, verifies holdings, and sends this data to PRLC for inputting. This is in accordance with the State Library's requirement that all union list projects it funds must have the data input by a qualified vendor to insure consistency and quality control.

A third example of contract work by PRLC is the retrospective conversion of serial holdings for West Virginia University (WVU). Although WVU began participation in PaULS in 1981, not all of its serial titles had been converted to machine-readable form by 1985. As part of an overall retrospective conversion project, WVU determined it would provide for the conversion of any serial records not already online or not current. As sections of the library collection are selected for recon, the serials in that subject group are pulled and the pertinent data sent to PRLC for posting.

Similar union list activity has also taken place in Palinet. Like LVAIC, ACLCP (Associated College Libraries of Central Pennsylvania), TCLC (Tri-State College Library Cooperative), and NEPBC (Northeastern Pennsylvania Bibliographic Center) have been awarded LSCA funds through the SLP to participate in union list activities. These projects were designed to create local union lists in conjunction with retrospective conversions. Thus both local union list holdings for the participating institutions and PaULS records for the union list database have been created. The ACLCP project involved 16 academic libraries and the TCLC project 30 academic libraries—some in adjoining states. The NEPBC project called for the conversion and entry of approximately 7,200 titles and 16,200 holdings. The project also called for original cataloging of titles not found, and approximately 1,000 local data records (ldr) to be updated.

Currently the total union list funding support from the SLP stands at $581,592.00. Indeed, the development of the Pennsylvania Union List of Serials is due in large measure to the efforts and support of the State Library of Pennsylvania. (See Appendix A.)

Prices for contracted union list projects vary with editing and other requirements. However, the range to date for creating a local data record is $1.00–$1.75 and $.50–$1.00 for updating an existing ldr. The price generally includes labor, equipment, shipping, telephone contact, supplies, and other incidental costs but does not include any OCLC and/or network costs.[5]

PaULS ACTIVITY IN 1986

It seems probable that most PaULS participants still regard the union list as a project activity rather than as something which is best maintained on an ongoing basis as part of the daily work routines. This is illustrated in statistics gathered in February and March of 1986. During those 2 months 15 institutions in PRLC reported union list activity. Activity varied from a low of 1 to a high of 502. Of the 1,963 transactions during that period, 1,724 were made by 7 of the 15 institutions. Activity by the PaULS participants who are Palinet members was at a similar low level.

The low activity level led once again to the inclusion of PaULS into the program for the PRLC Spring Conference. Demonstrations were conducted by representatives of West Virginia University and Indiana University of Pennsylvania. This hands-on session provided conference attendees with some convenient and easy guidelines for updating their local data records. It must be noted, however, that the recent acceptance of the exception rule of entry for microform holdings did have an impact on the presentations.

Just prior to the PRLC 1986 Spring Conference, the Serials Management Committee held a special meeting regarding the use of E.6 and E.7 Exceptional Entry of Microform Serials found in Appendix E of the OCLC Serials Control User Manual.[5] The exceptional rule permits microform holdings to be attached to a bibliographic record for the serial in hard copy for union list purposes. The use of the exceptional rule, previously not PaULS policy, was reviewed when PRLC, as the PaULS union list agent, began to accept contracts for union list updating similar to those they held for retrospective conversion work.

Previously, PaULS policy was to follow established national standards as found in AACR2 and the standard for serial holdings at the summary level, *ANSI Z39.42*.[6] That policy meant that a separate bibliographic record was created for the hard copy and each separate microform version of each serial title. Holdings were associated with the appropriate bibliographic record. Although there has not been a definite resolution, PaULS policy has been relaxed to the point where each participant may choose either of the two options: following the standards in full or adopting the practice of exceptional entry. The latter has been adopted by the United States Newspaper Program and, at a minimum, newspaper holdings for PaULS participants will follow exceptional entry.

In February 1986 a special meeting of representatives of Palinet and PRLC was held. The representative of the State Library did not attend but had been involved in planning the meeting and was expecting recommendations for action from the group. Ruth Carter, who had served as Technical Director of the PaULS during its initial five years, was included as an advisor. It was agreed that a proposal would be submitted to the State Library of Pennsylvania for a small amount of LSCA funding to cover the cost of preparing and distributing an updated PaULS procedures manual. The one prepared as part of PaULS-3 was badly outdated. For example, OCLC restructured the search mechanisms for serials control users which made a difference in the default search capabilities. If a user did not specify the entire OCLC database, searching from a serials control log-on was restricted to titles held by an individual institution. Other changes to be made included the need to describe the exceptional entry option, provide guidelines for newspapers, and, in general, add improved examples.

A proposal was subsequently developed by a Subcommittee of the PRLC Serials Management Committee and submitted to the State Library in May 1986. At the same time, it was expected that the networks would develop training programs to be put into effect when the new manual is ready for distribution. In addition, the networks cooperated in publicity for the LC/RTSD Serials Institute held in Pittsburgh in October 1986. Since the Institute covered serials cataloging in depth, the networks decided to encourage PaULS participants in their respective areas to gain training on serial bibliographic record creation in that forum. Overall, few PaULS libraries have a large quantity of original serial cataloging. By focusing on the union list local record creation and use in network training, network staff can concentrate on the components of the process that involve the most participants.

THE FUTURE OF PaULS

Although major contract project efforts like those of LVAIC and WVU will make a significant contribution to union list efforts in the PRLC/Palinet services areas, they are not enough. Not only do some libraries need to complete conversion of their holdings to PaULS for the first time, many who entered data at the time of the core list activity have done no maintenance. And, many libraries still look upon maintenance as a project rather than as an ongoing process. Until the libraries in those categories make a commitment to PaULS as an invaluable shared database which achieves its optimum usefulness when it is maintained on a current basis, it will not fulfill its capabilities.

CONCLUSION

Carter and Bruntjen[7] listed issues that needed to be resolved to have a satisfactory transition from the development of PaULS to the maintenance of PaULS. In early 1987 most of those issues still exist. They are:

—the governance of PaULS,
—the organization of PaULS,
—the coordination of PaULS—both long-term and short-term,

— how quality control can be achieved,
— who will pay for PaULS, and
— provision for continued participation by non-OCLC libraries.

A few issues on the earlier list have been resolved in whole or part. One of those was the relationship of small union list groups to the whole. Because OCLC allows a variety of levels of union list offline products, profiling of a single institution in multiple union list groups, and subgroup profiling, subgroups of an overall list can define them to their requirements.

Offline products do not seem to be an issue at this time. Most use of the PaULS database as a whole is online. Microfiche and tap products have been ordered by individual participants or consortia but are not in demand for the file in its entirety. When PaULS offline products first became available in 1984, copies were produced in microfiche and distributed to participating libraries. Although valuable, there is insufficient demand to produce a new list on fiche. At the same time as the overall PaULS microfiche was produced, a printed copy of all of PaULS was ordered by PRLC. Copies of the printed version were offered for sale but there was little demand and there are no plans to make subsequent versions available for distribution. It is clear that the users of PaULS data prefer the online information.

Some of the maintenance issues probably will never be settled. However, it is encouraging that the networks and the State Library of Pennsylvania are united in support of PaULS. Their active efforts to educate, train, and promote PaULS should produce many positive results. The renewed participation of some of the core list libraries could enrich the database and its perceived usefulness. External circumstances such as the declining value of the United States dollar could force a re-examination of the serial purchases of many libraries. In such a case, PaULS provides an existing online mechanism for communicating cancellation information rapidly. That capability was described by Carter and Bruntjen[8] in a review of the PRLC Serial Cancellation Project that was funded by the Council on Library Resources.

One lesson that seems self-evident at this stage of PaULS is that there seems to be a critical mass factor involved in a library's commitment to maintenance of its holdings in PaULS. It appears to be unrealistic to expect ongoing maintenance to be high on an individual library's list of priorities unless it has all or almost all of its serials holdings entered into PaULS in OCLC. Therefore, the various projects such as those in LVAIC, ACLCP, and NICOP were necessary precursors to ongoing maintenance efforts. In many cases, PaULS participation is driven by local online systems and the need to convert serial bibliographic and holdings records to serve those systems. PaULS in those cases benefits incidentally. Once the data is in PaULS it becomes valuable for resource sharing and cooperative ventures. These factors, plus the constraints of money received from the funding source—the State Library of Pennsylvania—operate to encourage, if not demand, the maintenance of PaULS.

Another factor that will help to keep the database clean is the establishment of an annual fee for PaULS participation by PRLC. This fee will be assessed on PRLC non-members as well if PRLC is responsible for the maintenance of the institutions holdings in PaULS. Those that do not want to pay the annual fee will no longer be considered PaULS members. The concept of an annual fee for PaULS membership is not entirely new. Palinet has had a fee for years. However, it is applied only to the OCLC libraries that are both Palinet and PaULS members.

PaULS exists today; it will exist tomorrow. It is already providing a service to library users in making the availability of serial resources known. In addition, library administrators, collection development staff, and others can benefit from a strong, comprehensive, and current database on the serial holdings of PaULS participants. With determination and commitment PaULS can fulfill all of its potential, not just some. That will occur when maintenance is accepted as the routine and not seen as the exception. Maintenance is neither easy nor inexpensive nor glamorous, but it is essential. In facing maintenance issues, PaULS is not alone. The CONSER participants meeting in November, 1986 changed the name of the CONSER Project to the CONSER (Cooperative Online Serials) Program. PaULS, and other large online union lists, must leave the project concept behind and commit to the program to achieve fully their promise for tomorrow and beyond.

REFERENCES

1. Ruth C. Carter and Scott Bruntjen, "The Pennsylvania Union List of Serials: Initial Development," *The Serials Librarian*, 5: 57-64, Spring 1981.
2. Ruth C. Carter and Scott Bruntjen, "The Pennsylvania Union List of Serials: Continuing Development," *The Serials Librarian*, 6: 47-55, Winter 1981/Spring 1982.
3. Ruth C. Carter and Scott Bruntjen, "The Pennsylvania Union List of Serials: From Development to Maintenance," *The Serials Librarian*, 8: 55-67, Summer 1984.
4. Timothy J. Sperry, editor, *Pennsylvania Union List of Serials Procedures Manual*. (Pittsburgh: Pittsburgh Regional Library Center, 1982).
5. *Serials Control: User Manual*. (Dublin, Ohio: Online Computer Library Center, 1983.) p. A29-A30.
6. American National Standards Institute, *American National Standards for Serial Holdings Statements at the Summary Level, ANSI Z39.42–1980* (New York: ANSI, 1980).
7. Carter and Bruntjen, "From Development to Maintenance," p. 59.
8. Ruth C. Carter and Scott Bruntjen, "PRLC Serials Cancellation Project," *Library Resources & Technical Services* 28: 299-307, October/December 1984.

APPENDIX A
UNION LIST FUNDING
STATE LIBRARY OF PENNSYLVANIA
PaULS FUNDING

PaULS-I	1979-1980	$99,304.00
PaULS-II	1980-1981	$99,804.00
PaULS-III	1981-1982	$91,000.00
PaULS-IV	1982-1983	$61,687.00
PaULS-V	1983-1984	$29,206.00

Total PaULS Funding $381,001.00

CONSORTIA PROJECTS

Philadelphia Academy of Natural Sciences	$19,060.00
Tri-State College Library Cooperative (TCLC)	$19,870.00
Associated College Libraries of Central Pennsylvania (ACLCP)	$56,000.00
Northeastern Pennsylvania Bibliographic Center (NEPBC)	$37,249.00
Lehigh Valley Association of Independent Colleges (LVAIC)	$45,512.00
Northwest Interlibrary Cooperative of Pennsylvania (NICOP)	$1,400.00
Carnegie Museum of Natural History	$9,750.00

Total Project Funding $183,841.00

OTHER MAINTENANCE PROJECTS

Revised Edition of the Union List Manual $11,750.00

Total State Library Support as of December 31, 1986 $581,592.00

Steps Toward an On-Line Union List

Ruth C. Carter, MA, MS

SUMMARY. This paper describes the on-line union list file currently being developed by the University of Pittsburgh and other libraries of the Pittsburgh Regional Library Center. Present procedures and future plans are described. The on-line holdings format for local data records agreed upon with OCLC is reported. It is expected that concepts worked out for the Pitt/PRLC on-line union list records will be precedent setting for other future on-line union list efforts.

As of December 1977, the University of Pittsburgh (Pitt) libraries and the other libraries of the Pittsburgh Regional Library Center (PRLC) are well on their way to having an on-line union list file of serial records. The file will be maintained as one part of the Ohio College Library Center (OCLC) on-line data base. Because the file is, in part, widely available through OCLC, Pitt and PRLC would like to share some of the background and developments to date, even though the situation is evolving rapidly. Furthermore, to reassure users of the serial records in the OCLC data base, such as Saxe, it seems important to state clearly the efforts being made to bring those Pitt and PRLC bibliographic records that are minimal up to full cataloging standards.[1]

Reprinted with permission of the American Library Association, taken from *Information Technology and Services* (Jan. 1978) by Ruth C. Carter. © 1984 and 1978 by ALA.

The author appreciates the support and contributions of many individuals both in making this project possible and in preparation of this paper. They include Glenora E. Rossell, director of university libraries, University of Pittsburgh; Florence M. McKenna, coordinator for processing, University of Pittsburgh; and Stephen B. Folts, executive director, Pittsburgh Regional Library Center.

HISTORICAL BACKGROUND

The University of Pittsburgh and PRLC union list files were developed in machine-readable form in the late 1960s and are presently stored on magnetic tape. The Pitt file, which contains the holdings for thirty-one locations, is maintained locally on a current basis. However, the PRLC file, which encompasses holdings for fifty-seven libraries, was last updated in 1973. Although they are similar in nature, there were enough differences, both in content and in choice of entry (as well as some variance in practice between latest versus successive title cataloging), to justify separate files at the time of the last simultaneous update for publication in 1973. Programming and computer time for that update were provided by the University of Pittsburgh. Because both files were designed prior to the development of LC-MARC-S, they are tagged differently and are in uppercase only.

Despite such limitations, much of the bibliographic data was more complete than those in other sizable union lists available in early 1974. In particular, publication dates and places of publication were ordinarily present. This was a key factor in OCLC's decision to use the Pitt and PRLC files. OCLC and PRLC signed an agreement that called for OCLC to convert the bibliographic information from the two files to MARC format. In addition, OCLC agreed to convert the Pitt/PRLC holdings information to local data records.

Shortly after the OCLC/PRLC contract was signed, the Minnesota Union List of Serials (MULS) became available to OCLC. MULS was a larger file (approximately 75,000 titles as compared with approximately 45,000 unique titles in the Pitt/PRLC files) and was in MARC-S format with upper- and lowercase. At the same time, the CONSER project was being organized, and OCLC gave priority to the addition on-line of the MULS file as part of the CONSER project. These on-line records became available in August 1975 and were followed shortly afterward by LC-MARC-S records and others. This is well documented in the literature by Anable, Upham, and others.[2,3]

CONSER diverted OCLC's interest in the bibliographic information in the Pitt/PRLC records as an initial serials data base. However, because of the existing OCLC/PRLC contract for the conversion of the Pitt/PRLC files, there was strong reason to pursue the projected on-line union list. In June 1976 the bibliographic records unique to the Pitt file (approximately 13,000) were added to the on-line data base. They had been checked at OCLC for duplication against the MULS file but not against the rest of the data base. Later in the fall of 1976, the PRLC unique records and PRLC/Pitt duplicates were converted. In addition, the Pitt and PRLC symbols were added to MULS records as appropriate.

GOALS AND OBJECTIVES

There are several reasons why the University of Pittsburgh and PRLC are interested in pursuing an on-line union list. An initial factor was the desire to provide for the maintenance of the file in a way that would enable regular production of printed output both of the file as a whole and as separate lists for each library. It was a definite objective to provide a single merged list of the Pitt and PRLC records. As mentioned previously, in the past this was not readily feasible, due in part to differences between successive and latest title cataloging. However, this problem should eventually be overcome with the on-line file. With current cataloging rules requiring successive entry and bodies such as OCLC and LC having expressed their intent to conform, the cataloging in the on-line file should at some point meet the specified standards.

A major benefit of an on-line file will be the obvious advantage of timeliness and more widespread availability of these up-to-date records. Early experience with the on-line file at Pitt indicates that a significant number of incoming interlibrary loan requests will be answered by the on-line file, because Pitt's most recent printed union list with its semi-annual supplements is not as current.

Another possible benefit will be the option of building a subject index to the union list. At a later date, Pitt/PRLC expects to receive tapes from OCLC that can be used to produce a printed union list. These tapes will be in MARC-S format and will contain a full bibliographic record for each title as well as holdings. Consequently, the subject heading fields can be manipulated to produce a subject index, or, more generally, a broad subject list based on LC classification could be produced.

It is important to note that the assignment of subject headings and call numbers for periodicals was not done previously by either the University of Pittsburgh or many of the other PRLC libraries. However, since Pitt/PRLC will benefit from the efforts of others using the OCLC system, it seems only appropriate that classification and subject work be provided for those titles that Pitt/PRLC either holds uniquely or processes first. Therefore, all cataloging being input is complete cataloging, according to OCLC requirements. In general, sharing efforts in bibliographic control and making resources known are both objectives of participation in on-line file building.

As stated above, Pitt/PRLC expects to produce eventually a printed list from a tape of records to be furnished by OCLC. This printed list may take the form of conventional hard copy or it may be in another format such as computer output microform (COM). Despite the many advantages of an on-line file, there are also many advantages to a printed list, including distribution to libraries without OCLC terminals. Many libraries in the PRLC list are non-OCLC libraries, and Pitt has many departmental libraries that do not have terminals. In addition, many public service points in the main library do not have terminals at present. By having an on-line file with the capability of producing printed union lists, Pitt and PRLC expect to be able to satisfy the needs and requirements of their various participating libraries for access to this information.

HOLDINGS

After the conversion of the bibliographic records, the next step on OCLC's part was to convert the Pitt/PRLC holdings data. The Pitt file conversion was completed in May 1977, with the PRLC file scheduled for a later date. Originally, the plan was to create one local data record for each copy of each title. However, at a serials training session at OCLC in December 1976 and subsequently in conversation with OCLC staff, it became apparent that the OCLC system is capable of handling union-list-type holdings on one record per title per union list file. Multiple holdings can be shown in the retrospective holdings field (RTHD) by repeating subfields that can be used for union list holdings statements. These subfields are ≠a Location (Pitt is using the four-character OCLC code), ≠b Local Call Number, ≠v Holdings, ≠y Dates, ≠e Acquisition Status, ≠f Retention Policy, and ≠g Completeness of Holdings. The latter three have been defined by ANSI Z39 subcommittee 40 in a draft standard. They are not necessary for Pitt/PRLC purposes in the foreseeable future, but Pitt plans to use the ≠v subfield to express holdings as they are formatted in the present union list. Thus, in the Pitt file, the RTHD field for *Journal of Library Automation* is recorded as: RTHD PITT ≠v V1- PITL ≠v V1- ≠a PITH ≠v V1-5,6INC,7-8.

Pitt/PRLC staff considered the possibilities of one record versus multiple local data records from several viewpoints. Serials check-in is not a concern at present, whereas the purpose in using the system is to produce union lists. Considering additional uses and factors, such as public serving searching, file maintenance, or production of a printed list from the file, it seems better to utilize one screen to display a bibliographic entity. The capability to produce a printed or COM list is important, because not all libraries represented in the file have easy access to the OCLC system. In addition, the Pitt/PRLC agreement with OCLC calls for OCLC to furnish Pitt/PRLC with a tape suitable to use for the production of a printed list. If desired, data could be extracted from one record if printed lists are desired for individual participating libraries. Although serials check-in cannot be done on one record serving as a union list record, Pitt or PRLC libraries that want to use it for check-in are still able to use the system to create individual local data records as required. In the future, it is possible that programming will be available by OCLC to take holdings data in individual local data records and display these together as one record. Thus, maintenance of a union list record would be strictly optional.

Another factor affecting the Pitt/PRLC preference for union list records is that the tape to be furnished to PRLC eventually will come from the on-line file rather than archival records. This means that bibliographic data originally in an on-line Pitt/PRLC record may be deleted when a CONSER participant (including LC, NSDP, and NLC) works on the record. Thus, it would not appear in a tape taken from the on-line file. For example, local area study codes such as LA (Latin America) originally converted by OCLC to a 651 tag would be deleted. The Pitt control number for the union list file is sometimes removed. Less computer storage space will be used by having one screen per title for each of the two files, because the constant data will not be repeated. It will also facilitate programming, because multiple holdings records will not need consolidation. One record will be especially helpful in inputting new local data records because it will be faster. It has been decided to place the Pitt and PRLC union list control number in Remarks (RMKS). The Pitt area study code will go into Location (LOCN). If it is an item classified in the Pitt library system, the call number will be placed in the ≠b subfield following the first ≠a subfield in RTHD.

UNIVERSITY OF PITTSBURGH
DEVELOPMENTS AND PROCEDURES

Pitt has been working with serials in the on-line system for some time. Beginning in November 1974, original cataloging has been input for new titles processed, if there was no existing record on OCLC. Starting in the fall of 1976, local data records have been created for holdings information. The Pitt file that was converted by OCLC was current through August 1975. Pitt furnished OCLC with a tape updated through January 1977. When OCLC converted the Pitt holdings statements, it was able to use the 1977 holdings data for those records on the 1975 tape. However, local data records for all bibliographic records new to the file between August 1975 and January 1977 had to be created by Pitt.

In order to form a basis for judging what would be involved in creating local data records according to the full specifications in the OCLC serials control manual, the Pitt serials staff experimented for six months with creating one local data record for each copy of each new title. Experimentation included use of the Definition (DEFN) field as well as complete detailing of the Retrospective Holdings (RTHD) field. As stated previously, the creation and use of multiple records were found to be unwieldy, and the development of the union list record was requested. Holdings input for Pitt has been in union list format since March 1977.

In order to establish and maintain an on-line union list file, the

University of Pittsburgh is working with three types of updates to the file. The same procedure will be used when PRLC begins active work (probably in the winter of 1978). The update types are (1) new bibliographic record plus associated holdings, (2) changes to holdings or other data, and (3) upgrading the bibliographic records for the file that were converted by OCLC from the old union list. The activity divides into current operations and a special retrospective project. It should be noted that the University of Pittsburgh is currently maintaining its present in-house union list system and will be using that system to produce printed supplements to its June 1976 edition until it is possible to produce printed output from tapes furnished by OCLC. The union list is a particularly vital tool in the Pitt library system because the majority of serials is not classified and does not appear in the card catalogs.

Following is a brief description of procedures presently employed:

I. New items.

Reporting libraries submit a photocopy of the title page and table of contents along with holdings and acquisitions information for each new title they receive. Photocopies of title pages accompany a Serials Action Form (see Figure 1). When information on a new title is received centrally by the Serials Unit, it follows procedures for searching and verification. Cataloging for the title, which may be original, LC copy, or other copy, possibly upgraded, serves as the basis for entry into the present off-line union list file and also the on-line file.

II. Holdings changes.

These are first entered in the present union list and then are held for updating the on-line file. Incoming holdings changes for records automatically created by OCLC are being accumulated for processing against the on-line file. Holdings are formatted similarly in both the on-line and off-line union list records.

III. Upgrading the bibliographic records.

About 13,000 records from the Pitt union list were loaded into the OCLC data base as unique bibliographic records. At Pitt's request, OCLC has listed these one title per page to use as

PITT-1971 (REV. 3/76) SERIAL ACTION FORM - UNIVERSITY LIBRARIES

TO _____ DATE _____

FROM - (NAME) _____ | DEPARTMENT _____

TITLE - (PUBLICATION) _____

OBTAINED BY:
____ SUBSCRIPTION   ____ EXCHANGE | PRINTOUT NUMBER _____
____ GIFT   ____ OTHER

NOTE: ATTACH A XEROX OF TITLE PAGE OR OTHER APPROPRIATE DATA

ACTION TO BE TAKEN

☐ TITLE CHANGE (SEE OLD TITLE ABOVE; NEW TITLE IN REMARKS)

    SOURCE OF CHANGE _____
    LAST VOL. (OLD TITLE) DATE _____ ISSUE NO. _____
    FIRST VOL. (NEW TITLE) DATE _____ ISSUE NO. _____

☐ ESTABLISH ENTRY ON PREVIOUSLY   ☐ CHANGE HOLDINGS AS INDICATED BELOW
    UNVERIFIED TITLE

☐ RECEIPT OF BACK ISSUES   ☐ CHANGE OTHER INFORMATION IN PRINTOUT
                                                             AS INDICATED BELOW

☐ RECEIPT OF FIRST ISSUE (VOL. NO. _____ DATE _____).

REMARKS: _____

FIGURE 1. Serial action form

worksheets. The titles are being searched one by one against the OCLC data base to determine if it contains more complete records. If a more complete record is found, the note "DO NOT USE THIS RECORD FOR CATALOGING – SEE OCLC # " is being added to the Pitt record. Then the Pitt holding symbol is transferred to the more complete record. Notification of the "DO NOT USE" action is sent to OCLC. If there are no other holdings attached to the record, OCLC will delete it from the on-line data base.

PRLC PLANS

The PRLC file has not been updated since 1973. Recommendations are presently being developed for procedures for the on-line updating and maintenance of the PRLC union list. Efforts are underway to secure funding for necessary staff. PRLC is anticipating centralized updating of the union list file. All records for the file will have the PRLC symbol (QPR) plus the symbol of each OCLC participating library added to the record. All updates for the union list will be submitted to a central location. Libraries will be able to submit updates via a form similar to Pitt's that will ask for OCLC number, title, and update information. New entries will be reported with sufficient data for cataloging.

All bibliographic records held by any PRLC union list participant should have the QPR symbol. The RTHD field in the local data records will contain in ≠ a subfields either the OCLC symbol of participating libraries or a subcode under QPR, such as QPR2, for libraries without OCLC terminals. An example is given below for *Platinum Metals Review*, an on-line PRLC record held by eight libraries.

Platinum metals review.
ISSN: 0032-1400 OCLC no. 1762481 Frequn: q Regulr: r
   Hld lib: QPRR Copy: Repr: Subsc stat: A Loan:
      1 CLNO
      2 LOCN
      3 FUND
      4 RMKS 6444900000

5 DEFN ≠v vol. ≠p no.
   6 NEXT
Date recd:
   7 CRHD
   8 RTHD QPRR≠v (1)– ≠y 1957– ≠a CPLL≠v 1– ≠y 1957– ≠a PMCC≠v 1– ≠y 1957– ≠a QPRE≠v 1– ≠y 1957– ≠a QPRK≠v 1– ≠y 1957– ≠a QPRX≠v 1– ≠y 1957– ≠a QPR8≠v 9– ≠y 1965– ≠a DUQQG≠v 1– ≠7 1957–
   9 CLMS
   10 BNDG

It should be noted again that using one local data record per title for a union list display for PRLC records will not preclude individual libraries from creating individual local data records for use as a check-in record. This will be possible because, as indicated above, both the overall QPR symbol and the symbols for individual libraries with OCLC terminals will appear on each bibliographic record.

CONCLUSION

Working toward an on-line list is a very challenging, demanding, and exciting project. Much of the speed of successful development depends upon attaining additional funding for staff, but some progress will continue even if limited by staff size.

Pitt/PRLC has not yet received a tape from OCLC to attempt to print a list. It will probably not request one until considerable updating of the union list file has been accomplished. When a tape is received, there will undoubtedly be a whole new series of problems. Some of these include the development of new programs for a tape in MARC-S format in contrast to the present tagging system, the lack of an easy way to develop the cross-reference structure available in the present list, and changes in entry records of which we are unaware (the file is so dynamic with the upgrading capabilities of CONSER participants that it is virtually impossible to be aware of all critical changes made). The decision will be made later on the form of printed output, and it will be determined, at least in part, by available funds.

Overall, Pitt/PRLC expects that, with careful planning, the investment in the development and maintenance of an on-line union list will be more than worthwhile. The staff is very enthusiastic about this effort, and the library administrators are extremely supportive of this innovative project that will improve library service to users throughout western Pennsylvania and northern West Virginia.

REFERENCES

1. Minna G. Saxe, "Great Faith and a Few Big Questions: Notes from a Librarian Using the CONSER Base," *American Libraries* 8:27, 42 (Jan. 1977).
2. Richard Anable, "CONSER: an Update," *Journal of Library Automation* 8:26-30 (March 1975).
3. Lois Upham, "Mixed Feelings: Taking part in CONSER," *American Libraries* 8:26-27 (Jan. 1977).

Cataloging Decisions on Pre-AACR2 Serial Records from a Union List Viewpoint

Ruth C. Carter, MA, MS

These remarks address decisions made on pre-AACR2 serial records from the standpoint of on-line union lists rather than from a concern for the internal records and catalog at the University of Pittsburgh.

Union lists have been undergoing many changes recently. One of these has been the incorporation of union lists into the on-line databases of major national utilities. This has necessitated union list agencies to undertake much more bibliographic work. As a result, bibliographic decisions made by these agents have become a subject of concern to a wide audience. Union lists developed on-line with OCLC or other bibliographic utilities must adhere to national standards for both holdings and cataloging. It is obvious that this is a significant shift in emphasis since heretofore union lists have traditionally dealt with minimal amounts of bibliographic data.

Adherence to these national standards is a basic commitment of the new Pennsylvania Union List of Serials (PaULS) which is on-line through OCLC. In addition, all work on the union lists of the University of Pittsburgh (Pitt) and the Pittsburgh Regional Library Center (PRLC) is being done in accordance with national standards. The Pitt and PRLC union lists are separate entities but both are incorporated into PaULS. It is understood that all new PaULS union list bibliographic records will be cataloged according to AACR2

Reprinted with permission from *Union Lists: Issues and Answers* (Ann Arbor: Pierian Press, 1982), pp. 77-80.

prescription including choice of entry and form of entry as well as bibliographic description.

The question being addressed presently is how are the pre-AACR2 serial records handled in union list processing? Before the decisions that have been made for PaULS are described, it is worth noting some general factors influencing cataloging for a union list.

USE OF A UNION LIST

First, it is necessary to review the essential purpose of a union list. That is its role as a *finding tool*. Secondly, by definition, a union list will include holdings for multiple libraries (whether multiple libraries within one institution or libraries from different institutions). Therefore, by necessity any union list entry may differ for a particular title from the entry chosen for that periodical in the records of one or more of its participants. This is just as true within one institution as among different institutions.

For example, the medical library at Pitt may choose to enter a particular publication under its title. Yet that same item might be entered according to its corporate entry in the records of one or more of the other libraries of the University. The key point here is that there is virtually no way a union list entry will exactly match internal choices for entry by all of its participants.

As stated previously, all new bibliographic records input into the OCLC database are cataloged in accordance with AACR2. From the PaULS vantage point, pre-AACR2 records already on-line fall into two major types: titles for which the only on-line record is latest entry cataloging, and titles for which there is a successive entry record or for which no title changes are involved. Policy decisions for the treatment of the pre-AACR2 records are described below.

OCLC LATEST ENTRY RECORDS

When a title has a latest entry record in the OCLC database and there is no existing successive entry record, a successive entry record for each related title held by a PaULS participant will be input. Successive entry records are created whether or not an existing latest title record is an authenticated or other CONSER record. The successive entry records will receive full AACR2 cataloging. This requires that the piece be consulted.

Again, that is a major shift in emphasis in union list work. In general, bibliographic activities and record selection are becoming central to on-line union lists. Cataloging from the piece means having the original publication or an acceptable surrogate (such as cover, title, page, table of contents, or publication statement). When title changes are involved, the first and last issue involved in each title change or the closest to each that can be located are consulted.

ADVISORY COMMITTEE RECOMMENDATIONS

It is important to note that the OCLC Serials Control Advisory Committee has strongly recommended that only successive entry records be used for union lists. This recommendation was accepted: *Addendum 1 Union Listing Capability* to OCLC's *Serial Control: Users Manual* states that "successive entry cataloging is mandatory for bibliographic level 's' records used for Union Listing."[1] In addition, that recommendation was transmitted to the CONSER Advisory Board. This type of standard for the selection of bibliographic records is necessary to achieve consistency among union lists. The fact that some of that effort may in some cases be decentralized makes such a standard inevitable.

The second general group of records contains those for which there is an existing successive entry record or records for titles not involved with title changes. When records in this category are found in the OCLC database, they will be accepted in the pre-AACR2 form if the record is complete.

If the title on-line is an incomplete record (these usually date back to earlier union list record conversion work), it will be upgraded on-line. And such upgrading must be in accordance with AACR2 (except for those records which have LC copy).

When such copy is available for the specific title in hand, it will be used to upgrade an existing on-line incomplete record. In those instances, only the form of name will be changed, not description or choice of entry. Certainly records in this category are a small percentage of titles. Nonetheless it was decided that for purposes of PaULS practicality in terms of time and effort have to be considered. The value judgment was made that it is probably more important to direct effort toward *adding new* items to the database rather than to *recataloging* items for which usable LC copy (not latest entry cataloging) exists.

MICROFORM HOLDINGS

Union lists of serials frequently include considerable holdings in microform. Many of the titles with microform representations have cataloging for the hard copy already on-line. Most of this, of course, is in a pre-AACR2 format. Because all new records of the OCLC database must be in AACR2 form, all records created after January 2, 1981 for serials in microform must also conform. This will increase the work required to produce a bibliographic record for microform serials. Despite the extra time required to produce AACR2 cataloging, it is accepted as part of the commitment of PaULS to conform fully to national standards. It is significant that both cataloging standards and the ANSI Summary Holding standards require separate records for original print items and their microform reproductions.

In summary, almost all current and retrospective work for Pennsylvania Union List of Serials including Pitt and PRLC union lists efforts will get AACR2 cataloging in the full sense. The basic exceptions to that are: (1) those cases when there is an acceptable successive entry record already on-line or (2) when an existing incomplete on-line record needs upgrading and LC copy for the specific title involved is available. In that case, the LC copy will be used to upgrade the record and the form of name will be changed when necessary.

NOTE

1. OCLC. *Serials Control: Users Manual*, A1:31, issued 8101.

Pittsburgh Regional Library Center Serials Cancellation Project

Ruth C. Carter, MA, MS
Scott Bruntjen, MA, MA, DA

SUMMARY. The Pittsburgh Regional Library Center Serials Cancellation Project originated as a result of substantial cuts in serial subscriptions by many libraries in western Pennsylvania in 1980. To make cancellation decisions and yet retain as broadly based a serials collection as possible in the region, the libraries attempted to communicate with each other in traditional nonmachine ways. Under development at the same time, the Pennsylvania Union List of Serials, a large, widely available database of bibliographic and holdings records, seemed to have the potential to communicate cancellation decisions as they occurred. This article reviews the history of the Serials Cancellation Project conducted by the Pittsburgh Regional Library Center with a grant from the Council on Library Resources. Technical details for implementing the project via the OCLC database are discussed and the findings of the project summarized. It was concluded that the use of large-scale online databases such as union lists of serials offers considerable potential to aid collection development officers and library managers.

INTRODUCTION AND BACKGROUND

In the spring of 1980, a cyclical phenomenon occurred in the libraries of western Pennsylvania. Although not limited to libraries in the economically depressed area of western Pennsylvania, those libraries, including libraries in or close to the city of Pittsburgh, were exceptionally hard hit.

Reprinted with permission of the American Library Association, "PRLC Serials Cancellation Project" (Oct./Dec. 1984) taken from *Library Resources and Technical Services*.

This recurring event was caused by the inadequacy of budgeted funds to cover the renewal cost of current subscriptions, much less any it might be deemed desirable to add. Therefore, there was a more or less simultaneous mandate in many libraries in the western Pennsylvania region to cancel existing serial subscriptions. The libraries included the University of Pittsburgh, Duquesne University, Carnegie-Mellon University, and the Carnegie Library of Pittsburgh, all of which had a tacit understanding and interdependence with each other regarding access to serial resources.

There were a number of factors behind the timing of the 1980 crisis. Some tended to be local in nature, such as institutional budget constraints, which made it difficult to increase monies for the acquisition of library materials; some were external, such as the decreasing value of the dollar in the world market. Libraries with a sizable percentage of subscriptions to foreign journals were particularly susceptible to a subscription budget that no longer covered existing commitments.

When the budget crises occurred, the library managers and collection development officers of the various institutions tried to coordinate the cancellation of journals. It was important to them that, insofar as possible, the only current subscription to any single title that existed in the region not be cancelled. Concern existed that the collective regional serial resources be as broad and comprehensive as possible.

Consequently, considerable attention was directed to attempts to find out which institution still held a given title and which titles any one institution might be considering cancelling. A number of methods were employed to exchange information on proposed or implemented serial subscription cancellations. These methods included: (1) meetings of library directors and collection development officers, (2) telephone calls, and (3) exchange of paper lists.

Lack of currency and/or limited distribution of the information were serious limitations of the methods to communicate actual or probable cancellations. At the very same time that cumbersome methods were being employed to coordinate the serial cancellation crisis, a powerful online tool, which could be used to transmit this and other collection development information on a current basis to a widespread audience, was in development. This was the Pennsylvania Union List of Serials (PaULS).

The development of PaULS has been described in detail by Carter and Bruntjen.[1,2,3] PaULS was funded with LSCA monies by the State Library of Pennsylvania. Active work on the Pennsylvania Union List of Serials began in the fall of 1979. It had significant impact early because it incorporated the existing online union lists of the Pittsburgh Regional Library Center (PRLC) and the University of Pittsburgh. In the spring of 1980 there were already more than forty thousand titles with holdings online. The holdings were displayed in Local Data Records (LDRs) and indicated which specific volumes were held by an institution. A holdings statement could include note information and later the ANSI codes contained in the *American National Standard for Serial Holdings Statements at the Summary Level*.[4]

Staff of the Pittsburgh Regional Library Center and the University of Pittsburgh were actively involved in the development of PaULS. It seemed to them that it had many as yet untapped or barely tapped potential applications. One of these was the capability of communicating cancellation decisions as they were made.

This paper describes the process by which the idea to use online union list information to aid collection development officers and library managers was funded, tested, and analyzed.

PROPOSAL DEVELOPMENT

When the idea occurred that the large-scale online union lists of serials are a natural mechanism for the communication necessary to maintain a broadly based regional serial collection, the next step was the identification of an appropriate agency to fund a pilot project. The Council on Library Resources (CLR) was approached because of its expressed interest in related applications that might receive widespread adaptation in regional and national academic and research libraries.

In response to an initial letter of inquiry, CLR staff indicated that they were interested in a pilot project. CLR requested that PRLC demonstrate that the problem to be addressed, in this case coordinating serial cancellation decisions as one portion of cooperative collection development, would have widespread applicability and utility if results were positive.

The next step was to telephone or write librarians at geographically dispersed institutions to inquire as to the utility of developing an online system of communicating cancellation of serial subscriptions. In addition, relevant literature was examined. Although there was no clear record of any previous attempt at communicating collection development decisions in an online mode as soon as they were made, there were previous attempts at coordinating serial cancellation decisions on a regional or type-of-library basis. Medical libraries were in the forefront of this type of cooperation. C. Lee Jones in his tenure as medical librarian, Columbia University Medical Center, advocated regional cooperation in serials acquisitions by medical libraries.[5] Many of his suggestions were implemented by the Regional Coordination of Biomedical Information Resources (RECBIR) program.[6]

Documentation to support demonstrated need and utility of an online mechanism for communicating cancellation decisions as they are made was an integral part of the proposal letter submitted to CLR on February 19, 1981. Subsequent discussion resulted in a revised budget conveyed in a letter of April 3, 1981. On April 30, 1981, the Pittsburgh Regional Library Center received the letter from CLR awarding the grant to carry out the work described in its earlier letters.

Essential to the proposal to CLR was a preliminary agreement with OCLC regarding the use of its system to communicate serial subscription cancellation decisions. Project developers approached OCLC with a preference to indicate a cancellation decision via the use of a code in the "Acquisition Status Code" field of summary holdings. Unfortunately, the code suggested, an 8, was not part of the existing *American National Standard for Serial Holdings Statements at the Summary Level*.[7] OCLC personnel concluded that use of the code was unacceptable because it did not follow existing national standards. Ultimately, it was agreed that the cancellation decision would be communicated in the form of a note in the fields for holdings statements.

Shortly after news of the award was received, one of the authors participated in a meeting of OCLC's Union List Task Force. At that meeting on June 1, 1981, it was agreed that subfield n of the SCHD and SIHD fields of the OCLC Local Data Records would be used to record the cancellation decisions. The wording adopted was:

cancellation effective with (vol):(no) (year):(month)
for example:
cancellation effective with 9:6 1981:12

The issue and the date cited are those of the last issue received.

While technical details for transmitting critical information were being agreed upon for use within the OCLC system, the PRLC Serials Cancellation Project was seeking other key participants. Temple University, Pennsylvania State University, and Marshall University agreed to participate with the other PRLC contributors to the Pennsylvania Union List of Serials.

An advisory committee to the project was formed with the following members: Susan Brynteson, University of Delaware; Hendrik Edelman, Rutgers University; Barbara Markuson, Indiana Cooperative Library Services Authority; Marilyn Norstedt, Virginia Polytechnic & State University; George Parsons, Council on Library Resources; Ruth Carter, University of Pittsburgh; and Scott Bruntjen, Pittsburgh Regional Library Center.

DESCRIPTION OF THE PROJECT

Originally, the project was scheduled for the period from August 1, 1981, through October 31, 1982. Its active work was eventually extended through December 31, 1982. The final report on the Serials Cancellation Project was submitted in December 1983.[8]

In August 1981, with the project formally under way, selected libraries were invited to be part of the cancellation project. Temple University and Penn State were participants in some of the initial stages of the Pennsylvania Union List of Serials but, as RLIN libraries, were not committed to comprehensive input of their serial collection data into PaULS. Marshall University, as a West Virginia library, was outside the initial focus of PaULS. All Pennsylvania libraries that were members of PRLC and also PaULS participants were requested to report cancellation decisions for serial subscriptions as those decisions were made.

In essence, the project consisted of asking participating libraries to notify PRLC of decisions to cancel serial subscriptions as soon as they were made. This requirement recognized the fact that a cancellation decision could be made but that it would often be a year or more before the last issue of a subscription would be received in the library. A second reporting step was absolutely essential.

Apparently, for a combination of reasons, it was not easy for participants to grasp the fact that cancellation decision recording, if it were to be useful for collection development purposes in a live situation, means two-step reporting. Many libraries that were requested to report cancellation decisions as they were made reported closed holdings or reported open holdings but then did not report closed holdings when the last issue arrived. The lack of general understanding of the purpose of the two-step reporting limited the overall usefulness of the actual project. However, it must be made clear that the two-step reporting is clearly an important and necessary step for cooperative collection development using online tools. Communication of that information is essential if these applications of online tools are to give full value by providing correct information.

Although the capability existed for most participating libraries to enter cancellation decisions directly online, it was decided to centralize input for reasons of quality control and monitoring activity level during the pilot project. PRLC furnished reporting forms to all project participants. These were returned by participating libraries to the cataloger hired half-time for the project. The cataloger was located at the University of Pittsburgh. Part-time inputters assisted the cataloger with the input of holdings and necessary bibliographic records. More than twelve hundred cancellation decisions were posted in the course of the project. Titles cancelled by the University of Pittsburgh were input directly by staff there.

THE PROJECT ADVISORY COMMITTEE: STANDARDS

The advisory committee to the serial cancellation project met twice: November 30, 1981, and December 8, 1982. Both meetings resulted in valuable direction and/or assessment for the project.

In the first meeting the members spent a great deal of time discussing the relationships of the project to standards and considering how the workshops planned for the project could be made meaningful. The workshops were the easy part. The advisory committee suggested that materials be furnished to the workshop participants in advance so they could work through various exercises and come to the workshops with some hands-on experience. The project staff accepted this advice and the workshops benefited from this premeeting online experience of the participants.

The standards issue was a much more difficult area in which to accomplish specific project goals. It has already been noted that one of the original goals was a new status code within the "Acquisition Status Code" of the *American National Standard for Serial Holdings Statements at the Summary Level*. It seemed logical to the individuals who proposed the cancellation project that there should be a new acquisition status code created for serials for which the subscription cancellation had been entered but the title was still being received in the library.

In general, the advisory committee to the project concurred. In fact, its discussion led to a recommendation for the creation of four new acquisition status codes to aid collection development officers. These were:

2 Acquisition under consideration
3 On order, not yet received
7 Cancellation under consideration
8 Cancelled, last issue not received.

The above suggestions for acquisition status codes were submitted to ANSC Z39 Subcommittee E, which was in the process of working on standards for serial holdings statements at the detailed level. The draft standard which went out for a vote, however, did not include the addition of the above values to the "Acquisitions Status Code" list of values. However, the fact that the advisory committee authorized the recommendations recognized the potential of online bibliographic databases shared by many institutions for an active role in collection development.

One developing de facto standard did incorporate a mechanism for communicating cancellation decision information. This was the

"USMARC Format for Holdings and Locations," which was in the initial stages of being drafted at the time of the cancellation project.[9] Members of the advisory committee helped influence development so that the draft communications format included provision for cancellation decision information. It is likely that there will be increased interest in the question of communicating collection development decisions in a standardized fashion as the focus shifts in many libraries from acquisition of materials to provision of access regardless of location.

CANCELLATION PROJECT WORKSHOPS

Five regional workshops were conducted as part of the PRLC Serials Cancellation Project. These were hosted by the University of Pittsburgh, Mercyhurst College in Erie, Pennsylvania, Temple University, Pennsylvania State University, and West Virginia College of Graduate Studies.

Practice exercises sent to the registrants in advance provided basic training in searching the Pennsylvania Union List of Serials online in the OCLC database. They included information about searching other union lists available through OCLC and made it possible for a collection development decision maker to take into account the holdings for a title of concern that might be located outside of the immediate area.

Another important part of the pre-workshop materials sent to participants were two questionnaire, one on current serial acquisitions and the other concerning cooperative collection development issues. Together the two questionnaires asked for information on topics such as the following: number of serial titles currently received; the number currently purchased; the number acquired through gift or exchange; the number of serial titles cancelled in 1981 and in 1982; the number of new titles ordered in 1981 and 1982; other libraries consulted, if any, and how they are consulted in making serial cancellation decisions; the libraries, if any, consulted when adding a serial title; the usefulness of cooperative collection development decisions and tools; and the most appropriate mechanism for cooperative collection development decisions.

The workshops were well attended. There were approximately

125 persons overall for an average of 25 per workshop. Responses regarding general interest in or perceived value of online communication of serial subscription cancellation decisions varied on a regional basis. In the urban areas, for example the Pittsburgh area, where the libraries are physically close and there was a significant amount of walk-in patron use from one library to another, there was considerable concern regarding the communication of cancellation information and real interest in cooperative collection development. On the other hand, in a region with libraries more dispersed geographically, as in central Pennsylvania, there was less expressed desire for prompt communication of serial cancellation decisions. This input led to the project conclusion that if the serial is not held within a convenient distance of the potential user, it might as well be available via interlibrary loan as in another institution within the region.

Overall, the workshops were an important and significant part of the project. They made it possible to introduce what were, in some cases, new concepts to a large number of librarians in West Virginia and Pennsylvania. In some cases, the topic of conscious regional collection development was considered seriously for the first time.

PROJECT CONCLUSIONS

Members of the advisory committee of the PRLC Serials Cancellation Project reached a number of conclusions about the project. The conclusions, limited to that project and outlined in its final report, are:

1. Cancellation reporting is best appreciated as one part of overall collection management information;
2. The next time budgets are decreased, librarians will appreciate that the system is in place even if it has not been fully utilized previously;
3. In the short term, the value was perceived most readily in those areas where users can easily commute to other libraries;
4. It was an off year in which to test the utility of communicating cancellation decisions because the dollar was high and

most libraries did not cancel many serial titles during the project;
5. There is a widespread lack of sophisticated use of any online system outside the conventional, narrowly defined, subsystem-specific uses;
6. The majority of librarians do not seem to care whether they have a voice in developing new strategies for problem resolution;
7. There should be an established code in the ANSI standard for summary levels 2 and 3 to aid machine manipulation;
8. In general, participants better understood and appreciated the uses of online files for more than passive applications at the end of the project;
9. Technical procedures to implement the communication of serial cancellation decisions have been incorporated into the manual for the Pennsylvania Union List of Serials and should be incorporated into the procedures for other union lists for maximum effect;
10. Inclusion of the provision for cancellation information communication in the draft of the "MARC Communications Format for Holdings and Locations" may have been influenced in part by this project;
11. The project reaffirmed and emphasized the value of online technology as an aid to collection development;
12. The value of systematic reporting of cancellation decisions was demonstrated, and the procedure should be adopted by others;
13. The project helped raise the consciousness of librarians to the interrelationship of activities in various areas, and librarians appreciated this awareness of other areas;
14. The cost of actually maintaining the cancellation information is minimal;
15. The maintenance of up-to-date cancellation data will be facilitated by the capability for decentralized online maintenance;
16. Maintenance of cancellation data should become part of normal routines in libraries;
17. Applications such as entering cancellations move biblio-

graphic files from a passive position to that of an active applications tool; and

18. Library managers need greater awareness of the strength of online tools in managing their collections. This project has demonstrated that can be done.[10]

SIGNIFICANCE OF THE CANCELLATION PROJECT TO LIBRARIES

There are now widely available machine-readable bibliographic databases. These databases, including RLIN and OCLC, have many thousands of serial titles in their files. The PRLC Serials Cancellation Project was an attempt to demonstrate that large machine-readable bibliographic databases can support many applications. In this particular case, the application was that of using the serials database online with OCLC as an active tool for collection development and collection management.

The middle and late 1980s will see increasing emphasis on access to library materials rather than acquisition of those materials. Nevertheless, an item, to be accessed, must be held someplace. The best method of providing access to a given serial title depends upon the frequency of use in a particular institution. It may be acquisition by the local institution or regional availability or availability anywhere. After considering the most current information on the availability of a given title, a librarian must still decide either to acquire a specific title or to provide access to the title through the holdings of another institution. This issue was discussed by Carter in relationship to online services and collection development in serials.[11]

Communication of collection development decisions online, as was tested for subscription cancellation decisions in the project described in this article, is an important step in making optimum collection management decisions. The large-scale bibliographic databases have just begun to have their potential tapped in terms of special applications. The serial cancellation project represents an attempt to heighten the awareness on the part of collection development officers and library managers of a potentially valuable tool at their disposal.

The next time there is a widespread budget deterioration in a group of libraries accustomed to cooperating or among libraries in a particular geographic region or state, there will be a need to communicate in a timely, systematic manner the collection development decisions about serial cancellations. The librarians participating in the PRLC Serials Cancellation Project will be in a more favorable position then because there is a mechanism in place to facilitate the communication of their cancellation decisions. In the meantime, it is hoped that additional institutions will begin to use the online, shared databases for collection development information of mutual concern in today's environment of interdependence and cooperation.

REFERENCES

1. Ruth C. Carter and Scott Bruntjen, " The Pennsylvania Union List of Serials: Initial Development," *The Serials Librarian* 5:57-64 (Spring 1981).
2. _____, "The Pennsylvania Union List of Serials: Continuing Development," *The Serials Librarian* 6:47-55 (Winter 1981/Spring 1982).
3. _____, "The Pennsylvania Union List of Serials: From Development to Maintenance," *The Serials Librarian* 8:55-67 (Summer 1984).
4. American National Standards Institute, *American National Standards for Serial Holdings Statements at the Summary Level, ANSI Z39.42–1980* (New York: ANSI, 1980).
5. C. Lee Jones, "A Cooperative Serial Acquisition Program: Thoughts on a Response to Mounting Fiscal Pressures," *Bulletin of the Medical Library Association* 62:120-23 (Apr. 1974).
6. Regional Coordination of Biomedical Information Resources, *Final Report, Submitted to New York Metropolitan Regional Medical Program* (New York: June 30, 1976).
7. ANSI, *American National Standard for Serial Holdings Statements*, p.13.
8. Ruth C. Carter and Scott Bruntjen, *Serials Cancellation Project, a Final Report presented to the Council on Library Resources* (Pittsburgh: Pittsburgh Regional Library Center, 1983).
9. "USMARC Format for Holdings and Locations Draft 1/31/84," p.29.
10. Carter and Bruntjen, *Serials Cancellation Project*, p.20-22.
11. Ruth C. Carter, "Online Services and Collection Development: Serials," *Serials Review* 9:69-71 (Summer 1983).

Online Services and Collection Development

Ruth C. Carter, MA, MS

This essay relates one type of online service, with which I have worked closely, to another type of online service with which I have great familiarity as a user. The first type of online service is represented by the Pennsylvania Union List of Serials (PaULS). It is online through OCLC and gives the holdings for approximately 80,000 titles held by Pennsylvania and area libraries. As I will discuss later, the PaULS database, and other online serial union lists as well, have implications for collection development and collection management.

Of significance is the fact that PaULS is one of many union lists that are accessible through the same nationwide online service that offers both interactive access and dynamic updating.

The second type of online service is the online databases and they are the real focus of this essay. The question to be looked at is what impact, if any, the retrieval of journal citations through database searches is having on collection development in the area of serials. In attempting to review trends in this area, the serial citations retrieved through database searching will be looked at in relation to the titles in a library's own collection and to titles held in the local area, state or region. The use of PaULS as an online finding tool will be examined. Online union lists of serials as a means for communicating online collection development and collection management decisions will also be discussed. In addition, it is noted that

---

This paper is based on a talk presented at a meeting of the College and Research Libraries Division, Pennsylvania Library Association.
Reprinted with permission from *Serials Review*, 9(2). (Ann Arbor: Pierian Press), 1983, pp. 69-71.

online vendor serial services such as those offered by subscription agents have the capability to serve as one collection development tool.

SERIALS IN ONLINE DATABASES

An increasing percentage of currently published serials are represented in the online database services. In most instances the services provide a complete bibliographic citation plus an abstract as well as descriptors, various headings and subject codes. In some cases the content of the article is also online.

Serials represented in online database services may be in almost any language or subject area. It is clear that providing access to the serial literature through online services is growing and will continue to grow.

Theoretically, a library could hold no serial titles and only provide information access to them through various online services. The opposite extreme is for a library to attempt to hold all serial titles that might ever be cited. The reality, of course, is somewhere in between the two extremes and will vary according to size and type of library, economic conditions, resource sharing opportunities, agreements and the like. Even within a large institution there are variations from one subject area to another relative to the percentage of citations retrieved on average during a search and that which might be expected to be found in the collections of a given library.

In relating online services to collection development in regard to serials there are at least two question: (1) how does a library measure the effectiveness of its collections in meeting the demands of its patrons for access to journals cited in the results of database searches, and (2) what factors may a library consider in deciding how to treat the presence or absence of particular titles in its collection?

Immediate feedback from patron to librarian is, of course, one way of determining the adequacy of a library's collection relative to the demand for journals created in search results. This could be verbal and there are other strategies including questionnaires and surveys that can be employed. The most common tangible measurement of demand for a particular title is interlibrary loan requests that are generated. These interlibrary loan requests may be easy to fill or they may be for titles that are more difficult to locate. Any particular title may be only requested once over a period of many years by a single institution. Or, it may generate many requests.

In some cases the user may request that the full text, if available, be ordered through the online service. Although costly, there are libraries, for example some corporate libraries, that might prefer to rely on online services to provide the text for articles actually in demand rather than either acquiring or storing a greater number of titles; or, alternatively accepting the time delay built into interlibrary loans.

One librarian told me that interlibrary loan services have generally improved but this in turn has created a greater expectation of what the service should be. A patron who might gladly have waited two to three weeks or more in the past may now consider a week or less an unacceptable delay. An example here is the *Harvard Business Review*, which has just become available online. It is too soon, however, to determine the effect of this on collection development decisions.

A record of interlibrary loan requests, however, cannot affect collection development decisions unless the information is made available to those individuals in the library who make the collection development decisions. In a small library, and this can include a branch or departmental library of a large institution, the librarian monitoring interlibrary loan activities may be the same person who does the selection. He or she is also very likely to be the person performing the database searches and interacting with the patrons. In a large institution these functions are all likely to be performed by specialists.

If care is not taken, valuable information that could affect collection development decisions may not reach those who could act on it. Not only should titles often requested be passed on to appropriate selection personnel, but the source of the request should be noted. This will make it possible to relate particular titles to database searching.

There seem to be two basic approaches to how online services directly affect collection development, at least for serials. One science librarian has noted that the only time online services entered into collection development decisions was when the same title recurred many times in the search results and patrons wanted access to the journal. Titles in that category may be either relatively new titles or ones which previously did not receive much consideration.

Titles which generate a demand are then checked for availability in the University's holdings at large and then in the local area or region. Those that are not readily accessible will probably be acquired, funding permitting. In other words, this approach is to use database results to suggest titles which need to be considered for local acquisition.

A second approach to considering database search results in regard to collection development is to actively use all available online and other finding services to prevent having to acquire the serial locally. In this situation the focus is on NOT acquiring the title. This is a case where the availability of online finding tools such as large-scale union lists can have significant impact.

Potentially union lists can provide services far beyond that of a finding tool if decisions to place orders or to cancel subscriptions are also entered online. A librarian who has an active policy of not acquiring journals of a secondary to tertiary interest can utilize such online services as union lists or services provided by subscription agents to provide the indication that the title is held elsewhere and thus does not need to be acquired locally.

Results of online searches can also be useful in identifying weaknesses in the collection. If relatively few of the serial titles cited can be found in the collection, the library may need to place more emphasis on the area as a whole. Of course, the results of a single search are unlikely to be a significant factor, but a pattern established over time will probably generate close review of the area in question.

In some cases, the coverage of the online databases is so comprehensive that there is no way that even a large library can own all the titles that are included. A librarian with collection development responsibilities for educational subjects stated that it is impossible to acquire all titles covered in the databases commonly used in the field of education. Therefore, she has adopted the policy of actively encouraging interlibrary loan services by explaining and publicizing them more.

It is possible to do that because of the availability of interlibrary loan services through the OCLC and RLIN online systems. Responses to interlibrary loan requests for journal articles which are usually filled by photocopies, have been particularly satisfactory, at least in the area of education. The same librarian did note that when she makes selection decisions, the fact that a title is included in one of the online database services is a definite plus. Interlibrary loan requests would also influence in favor of title acquisition if the same title keeps recurring.

ONLINE AND FINDING TOOLS

I have reviewed some of the factors relating to collection development decisions in regard to database search results. One of the most basic considerations is access to any particular publication through another institution's holdings. Now I would like to consider briefly those online services which are basically finding tools to identify the location of the journal for which a citation has already been found. These finding tools may be at the level of institution identifier only, or may be specific to actual volumes held.

Online finding tools include the databases of the major bibliographic utilities including RLIN and OCLC. They also include services offered by several commercial vendors, primarily subscription agents, that are making information available on holdings of multiple institutions as well as acquisition or receipt data available only to a single institution.

The focus here will be on OCLC because it is the largest and most widespread of the online bibliographic search services. It is also especially noteworthy in its developments in the area of serials. One of OCLC's most successful developments has been in the area of serial union lists. It now has at least 20 union list groups committed to active file building through OCLC. One of these is the Pennsylvania Union List of Serials. As a conservative figure PaULS has approximately 80,000 titles and several hundred thousand holdings. It is growing daily. Other union lists such as the one for Indiana are already of a similar magnitude.

Until November 1982, PaULS was in the old format and did not interact directly with the other union lists on OCLC. However, at that time PaULS was converted to the format required for the union listing capability. With that occurrence, an OCLC user will be able to look for a serial title first in the union list group which is closest or in which the home institution participates, in our case the Pennsylvania Union List. If that search is unsuccessful, a simple command will display the holdings for another union list group for the same title, and if that is unsuccessful, a third group and so on.

The benefit to searching the union list files rather than looking for the title in the cataloging mode is that the union list displays include volumes held with appropriate years of coverage. Interlibrary loan requests can then be generated with a higher likelihood of being filled. This is so because there will have been an indication that the institution being asked to fill a request has the specific volume needed. OCLC plans to make it possible to interact directly between union listing and interlibrary loan. The elimination of extra log-on and log-off procedures should make the union listing data even more valuable than they already are.

UNION LISTS

Another way to make the online union lists even more valuable is to move them from a somewhat passive to an active role in collection development and collection management. A tremendous amount of time and money in Pennsylvania and throughout the nation has gone into file building. Much of the initial impetus for this in serials came with the CONSER project. The availability of OCLC's union listing capability has been a major factor recently. Now that large scale online serial databases are present, the capability exists to begin applications against the files.

It seems a logical extension of present union listing to record acquisition and deacquisition decisions in the online union lists. This could mean creation of a union list record when an institution has ordered a title. It could also mean recording an institution's decision to cancel a title at the time that decision is made. In most cases a cancellation decision will be made some time before the last issue is actually received in the library.

A pilot project to develop a mechanism for communicating cancellation decisions and measuring the usefulness of this communication as they are made has been conducted by the Pittsburgh Regional Library Center during late 1981 and 1982. The project has funding from the Council on Library Resources. A librarian attempting to make serial collection development decisions based on database search results or any other factor can certainly benefit from the inclusion of order and cancellation information in online finding services. They present the opportunity to communicate this information widely and on a current basis. It is particularly useful in location or regional settings where close accessibility to a journal title at another institution is most likely to be a direct influence on a library's decision not to acquire a title for its own collection.

It is clear that online services of all types are here to stay in libraries. Even if the actual technology changes, the concept of current availability of information with retrieval assisted by technology is certain to increase. How these online services affect future collection development decisions regarding serials will depend on a number of factors. One of these will be: how rapidly can the document in question be delivered?

Another issue will be whether or not searches can be limited by relating them on a priority basis. For example, it should be possible to retrieve only titles held by a given library on a first pass. Or retrieval of citations may be limited to titles held in the local area or region. Some searches, depending on the needs of the user, could continue to be comprehensive.

At present, a human is the primary interface between the online databases providing citations and the online services finding locations for the titles cited. In the future these are likely to be linked by machine or some other form of nonhuman interface. Combined with improved document delivery and machine-generated analysis of the results of database searches as related to use of the institution's own collection versus its interlibrary loan requests, it seems certain that online services will increasingly affect serial collection development in libraries of all sizes and types. Of course, it will continue to be a human who makes the ultimate collection development and collection management judgments.

Union Listing— A Tool for Reference Service

James D. Hooks, MLS, PhD

Librarians have experienced numerous changes in technical processes and information retrieval in recent years. The most significant changes relate in some degree to the computerization of library functions. Many librarians have seen the change from the older Library of Congress card order slips to the newer optical scan slips and eventually to computer produced cards. Academic libraries, for the most part, were among the strongest advocates of the new technologies. In many instances, academic libraries with their access to institutional computer facilities developed in-house programs to perform routine functions. However, without any suitable guidelines for standardized formatting, these in-house systems often were less than desirable for a number of reasons—poor planning, short-sightedness, computer limitations, etc. Once the library community and those responsible for funding library operations realized that the use of computers and computer systems by librarians was inevitable, the next logical step was to design or select programs which would serve both the institution and the library community. The gradual computerization of the union list illustrated this trend. The first significant effort with union listing did not occur until the first edition of the *Union List of Serials* in 1927. While both the first edition of the *Union List of Serials* and the subsequent second and third editions were monumental bibliographic projects, there was one persistent problem—even with supplements, printed lists quickly became outdated. Keeping track of new titles, cessations, cancellations, etc., is of major importance if accuracy in institu-

---

Reprinted with permission from *West Virginia Libraries*, vol. 38, no. 3 (West Virginia University, 1985).

tional holdings is to be maintained. The problem of up-to-dateness can now be resolved thanks to online computer technology and union listing options available through the OCLC Serials Control Subsystem. The union listing component, as described below, is an integral part of the serials subsystem. The local data record provides the basis for union listing:

> The Union List is designed to be copy specific. There must be a separate local data record for each copy of a title held. The OCLC system merges these local data records together to form a single union list display. The merging process is determined by the union list group or groups for which a library has been profiled. What this means it that, in addition to an individual institution's profile, participating libraries are given a common symbol under which their individual symbols are merged. All current OCLC libraries in Pennsylvania are profiled under the symbol PASU. If, for example, the Falk Medical Library joined a medical libraries union list group under the symbol MLUL, its holdings for a particular title would be retrieved by union list searches for either PASU or MLUL. In the OCLC Union List Display, the local data record does not stand alone. It is tied to a full serial bibliographic record. (Sperry 2)

Even though the OCLC Serials Control Subsystem addresses specific needs for serials librarians, the scope and parameters of union listing provide a database which can be utilized as an extremely effective access tool for patrons and public service librarians.

Libraries, like other social institutions, have undergone numerous changes since humble beginnings during colonial times. The prevailing attitude in libraries at that time was one of restriction. Borrowing books from the college library was often limited to faculty and upper classmen. Under these conditions, libraries had little concern, if any, for union listing or resource sharing. University libraries, in particular, tended to be quite restrictive and served the needs of a select few.

The twentieth century witnessed an accelerated growth and development of many technological advances. The information explosion placed strenuous demands upon libraries for resources and services. The rapid growth of library borrowing and lending during this time had a significant impact upon libraries. As one librarian noted, "by 1927 the practice of interlibrary lending had become common enough in the United States that a national interlibrary loan code was adopted to clarify and standardize policies and procedures" (Parker 871).

Not only did the demand for technical information increase, but also easy access to and rapid availability of these materials, mostly from serial publications, was expected. All of this diversity and specialization has resulted in the fact that no library can really stand alone anymore. Numerous reciprocal borrowing and lending policies have been developed, consortia formed, and information networks created so that libraries might better meet their growing obligations more efficiently. While future technology may make electronic information retrieval and delivery an everyday occurrence, the traditional interlibrary loan service is currently the primary method of obtaining requested materials.

In the interest of providing satisfactory interlibrary loan services and also maintaining fair use practices among libraries, interlibrary loan guidelines have been adopted to set forth the parameters of judicious interlibrary loan usage. *The Pennsylvania Interlibrary Loan Code* states, in general, that "interlibrary loans may be requested for any material which the borrowing library has identified as being in, or has strong reason to believe is in, the lending library's collection" (Pennsylvania 2). Since the patron's first concern is usually regarding the turnaround time, the borrowing library needs to be able to ascertain as accurately as possible the location of the needed material. The ILL Code further outlines reference and location procedures which libraries are obligated to observe when requesting materials:

> The Borrowing library will make every effort to locate the material requested through local, state and regional union catalogs, book catalogs, microfilm catalogs (such as the Union Library Catalogue of Pennsylvania microfilm), union lists; through interlibrary loan clearinghouses; through on-line and off-line bibliographic and cataloging systems (such as OCLC inc.); and through any other available sources. (Pennsylvania 5)

Accurate verification and location of requests contribute significantly to sound interlibrary loan services for both the borrowing and lending libraries.

The formation and subsequent growth of OCLC have made possible a more accurate and speedy degree of monographic verification than was previously possible with traditional tools. However, serial publications generally and union list holdings specifically have not undergone as much widespread development as monographic entries. Consequently, the lack of copy specific information in the union list format continues to hinder the location function in the interlibrary loan process.

One approach in bringing a union list to a more complete level was initiated at Indiana University of Pennsylvania. Katheryn Mallino, IUP Serials Librarian, and Ruth Carter, Union List Project Coordinator, being aware of the eventual necessity of local maintenance, agreed that obtaining some firsthand information about local maintenance would be beneficial to the promotion of local union list maintenance when it would become the responsibility of each participating library. It was agreed that IUP, with 3,500 active periodical subscriptions, should prove to be an adequate test site. A centralized network project was employed at the onset, and more recently, local maintenance has been initiated.

In 1978-1979, the PRLC union list project was just getting underway in the Pittsburgh Regional Library Center. The decision had followed that Indiana University of Pennsylvania would participate in this project and procedures to accomplish the work would have to be developed. By mid 1980, the Pennsylvania Union List project had begun to materialize. In a sense, two union list projects were simultaneously in process. Ruth Carter discussed this problem at the April 15, 1980 meeting of the Ad Hoc Committee on Union List of Periodicals. "The first year of the Pennsylvania Union List will entail a specific number of titles and a specific number of libraries both superimposed on the PRLC list" (Carter [1]). However, with funding from the Pennsylvania State Library, a PaULS (Pennsylvania Union List of Serials) project clearinghouse was established at the University of Pittsburgh and Ruth Carter was appointed project coordinator. By means of a questionnaire from 67 participating libraries (17 PRLC member libraries plus 50 additional, mostly from Eastern Pennsylvania), a core list of 2,200 titles was prepared and sent to participating libraries on June 5, 1980. Each library, with holdings on the core list, reported all copy specific information to the PaULS clearinghouse where the data base inputting was completed by trained personnel. It should be noted that the first PaULS core list was for paper holdings only. Microfilm holdings would be processed at a later date. In the meanwhile, PRLC blue slips were being accepted at PRLC headquarters for the PRLC union list project. The first call for PRLC blue slips went out on July 7, 1978 and continued until the cutoff date on May 31, 1982.

Although a great deal of holdings data was accumulating, there was a serious problem with the OCLC union list profile and concern regarding when the OCLC union list conversion would occur. By late 1979, OCLC began to experiment with possible union list profiles but it would be a year before OCLC's union list profile would be ready for final testing. In addition to the format problem, librarians were quick to note that the lack of linking capabilities between paper, microfilm and microfiche records would occasionally entail additional searching to determine an institution's complete holdings if held in different formats. This problem still persists even though some libraries have included notes in the LDRs (local data records). Somewhat related to the format situation was the lack of the 4th-letter display of an institutional OCLC symbol. Without this capability, it was not possible to immediately determine where, in a decentralized library, a particular title was to be found. Union list searching is the only OCLC program that currently provides a 4th-letter display capability. Other enhancements such as improved search keys and cross logging between the interlibrary loan and name address subsystems would further improve access to the union list. The most notable concern, especially of the Pennsylvania State Library, was the need for off-line products. The first such product was the production and distribution of the core list on microfiche generally referred to as COM (Computer Output Microfilming). The first COM union list was available in the fall of 1983, and with funding from the Pennsylvania State Library, 2,000 copies were distributed state-wide to both OCLC and non-OCLC libraries. In the spring of this year, both a second edition of the COM union list and the first edition of the paper union list were available. In the meantime, an important milestone would be observed when the 1973 PRLC printed union list (approximately 50,000 titles) would undergo OCLC conversion to an online data base. In mid 1982, a special core list was prepared and sent to special libraries and the PaULS micro core list was also prepared and sent to all participating libraries.

As the project proceeded, it was soon noticed how a computerized union list would relate to and enhance reference and interlibrary loan services. By late 1981, Dr. Scott Bruntjen, former PRLC Executive Director, observed: "the *Pennsylvania Union List of Serials* (PaULS), begun in late 1979, is now developed to the point that it should begin to make a positive contribution to your interlibrary loan work . . . with more than 75,000 titles and 300,000 holdings, this tool should go a long way toward satisfying serial interlibrary loans regionally." However, like so many other libraries, a shortage of terminals, staff and time restricted the development of any major plan of action for participation in PaULS at IUP. Normally, any retrospective conversion project is accomplished through vendors or some type of contractual basis. The utilization of dial access from the Armstrong County Campus Library eventually offered a viable short-term solution to the immediate problem. However, larger issues were before the PRLC Advisory Committee.

Even in the first year of PaULS, the Committee, under the leadership of Ruth Carter, began to address the question of future maintenance. Although the project had been initiated by participating libraries submitting union list report forms of specific holdings (known as blue slips), which were input at a central location, the time would come when each institution would have to assume local maintenance. There was general agreement that local maintenance would be the key to keeping PaULS viable; however, there were questions regarding its feasibility for some institutions. In order to better ascertain an answer to this, IUP was targeted to be an experimental site for local maintenance in order to provide some observable data which would address two main questions:

1. Was local maintenance feasible? And, if so, in what manner would it most likely occur?
2. Would dial access be adequate for union list inputting?

When IUP began its union list project, there were only two OCLC terminals in the main library which were primarily used by the cataloging and acquisition departments. Neither terminal was conveniently accessible for union list activity, nor was there much open terminal time during normal working hours. Dial access capability for union list purposes would provide a partial solution. Since the only available dial access installation then was at the Armstrong County Campus in Kittanning, located 28 miles from the main campus, it would be necessary to determine whether or not such a project could be managed from this remote location. Following a 30-day trial run, it was established that, with the employment of a part-time library assistant, the project could be undertaken. This temporary arrangement would last until a time when main campus would be able to assume the responsibility for maintenance. Union list management from a remote center was further facilitated by the existence of an in-house serials computerized program which was also accessible via dial access. This data link with main campus provided easy record verification when creating union list LDRs. When record verification could not be ascertained via the in-house serials program, it was necessary to contact the serials department via electronic mail or telephone and request verification usually requiring an actual inspection of the holdings.

The IUP experience demonstrated that local union list maintenance was possible with existing staff but with some modification, especially if additional staff time could not be provided. In most instances, local maintenance could be absorbed into the normal work flow. Each participating institution would decide which manner of maintenance best suited its situation. Inputting might be selective rather than comprehensive. Selectivity might be based upon unique holdings, indexed titles or other special criteria. Also, it was determined that dial access inputting (following OCLC's conversion to the union list format) was both possible and adequate.

Because union listing requires only a few basic OCLC commands, terminal operators were able to learn or make the transition to dial access with reasonable ease. Dial access users soon became both machine confident and machine competent—confident that dial access is reliable and competent in the use of OCLC equivalent commands. The most notable advantage of dial access is its versatility. It may be used to access other computer systems and data bases such as DIALOG.

At IUP no major problems were encountered in updating holdings in PaULS via dial access. The one notable inconvenience is the absence of any insert capability to add or change one or more characters in a field. Rather, the whole field must be rekeyed. Except for complicated holding statements, however, this was hardly noticed. During most months an average of 200 IUP local data records are reviewed. Some require change of data or need to be deleted. Others are verified as accurate LDRs. Verification of existing records had been considered important because of the different tape loads and machine conversions involved in the initial creation of PaULS. This step will not be required for existing records on an ongoing basis.

Although the Reference Department is rarely the first to receive an OCLC terminal, the use of OCLC in reference/interlibrary loan service is reasonably well established at this time. Union list access enhances reference/interlibrary loan service by making "copy specific" information available for patron referral or interlibrary loan transactions. Interlibrary loan requests at IUP are about three to one in favor of periodicals. If this pattern is typical among libraries, then the creation of a broad-based and well-maintained union list has definite potential. Also, the union list concept has significantly improved ILL service by providing accurate lending locations and ultimately decreasing the turnaround time. Patrons in or near to metropolitan areas may have the option to use other institutions where referral is clearly more satisfying for the patron when copy specific information is available.

The online union lists are most valuable when the records are updated on a current basis. The experiences at IUP indicate that even dial-up users of OCLC can provide local maintenance on a timely basis and with ease.

BIBLIOGRAPHY

Bruntjen, Scott. Letter to library directors [and] interlibrary loan librarians. 11 November 1981.

Carter, Ruth. Ad Hoc Committee on Union List of Periodicals. Minutes. [Pittsburgh]: PRLC, 15 April 1980.

P[arker], R[alph] H[alstead]. "Library Science," *Encyclopedia Britannica: Macropaedia*. 1974 ed.

The Pennsylvania Interlibrary Loan Code. Adopted by the Interlibrary Loan Code Development Group, February 13, 1979. Harrisburg: State Library of Pennsylvania, 1979.

Sperry, Timothy J., ed. *Pennsylvania Union List of Serials Procedures Manual*. [Pittsburgh]: Pittsburgh Regional Library Center, 1982.

West Virginia Union List— A Need Fulfilled

Mildred Moyers, MA, MLS

SUMMARY. In 1962 the need for integrating library service was foreseen as necessary to provide a sound basis for improving resources and services within the state of West Virginia. The *West Virginia Union List* proved to be the vehicle by which this goal was to be accomplished. In this article, the development of a library cooperation project is traced from its beginnings a quarter of a century ago to the introduction of present-day online systems.

For some time union lists have provided the finding tool used by institutions or libraries to locate serial titles and holdings. Likewise, a union periodical list representing the periodical collections of a group of cooperating libraries was designed to facilitate the sharing of bibliographic resources. The concern for better utilization of the limited resources in West Virginia was evident among librarians and researchers a quarter of a century ago. It was the need for cooperative use of resources, especially through interlibrary loan, as well as problems of the cost of technical and scientific publications and limitations of the space necessary to store and maintain large collections that eventually resulted in the undertaking of a union list project at West Virginia University.

HISTORICAL BACKGROUND

The concept of the *West Virginia Union List* had its beginnings in 1962 when Michael M. Reynolds[1] foresaw the need to integrate

---

Mildred Moyers is Chief Bibliographer and Assistant Professor of Library Science at the Wise Library of West Virginia University, Morgantown, WV 26505-6069. She is Editor of the *West Virginia Union List* (1972-) and a member of the OCLC Serials Control Advisory Committee and the PRLC Serials Management Committee.

library service in West Virginia. Through his efforts in determining what librarians and library users wanted and how library service could be disseminated throughout the region, he surmised that one of the first things needed was a list of the available scientific, technical, and social science serials. These areas were represented by strong collections in the West Virginia University Libraries. Jointly, the National Science Foundation and West Virginia University Library sponsored a union list project. As a result, the first computerized issue of *Union List of the Scientific, Technical and Social Science Serials in the West Virginia University Libraries* was published in October 1962 to provide a means of indicating what materials were actually available in the region for study and research. Major bibliographic tools available at West Virginia University were also included. Omitted from the issue were serials the parts of which were cataloged as separate works, less used United States government publications, and incomplete volumes of serials.

This initial cooperative effort was intended to provide a sound basis for the provision of better resources and services in the region and thereby allow smaller libraries an opportunity to serve more effectively the needs of their users.

The introduction to the first edition stated that "the *Union List* should not be considered as an end in itself—but rather a first step in an investigation to find ways to make the most effective use of resources."[2] Since interlibrary loan and the need for research information were central to the problem of integrating library resources, the publication was an initial attempt to broaden and expedite West Virginia University lending and reference services. Even in 1962, it was hoped that the *Union List* would be enlarged to include serials not in the University collections. The goal was to integrate library service in the region and develop a library cooperation project that would provide through resource sharing a sound basis for the improvement of resources and services in the region. Keeping this goal in mind, West Virginia University began in January 1963 an experimental service to provide free-of-charge copies of short articles from journals or serials to educational institutions in the region.

Second and third editions of the *Union List*[3] were published in 1964 and 1965, respectively. These two editions were still supported in part by the National Science Foundation grant. By 1966, the vision of enlarging the *Union List* to include holdings not in the University collections became a reality. The 1966 edition, revised by Lorise Boger[4] and published by the West Virginia University Library under the present title of *West Virginia Union List*, included 15 cooperating libraries in West Virginia in addition to the 4 West Virginia University Libraries. The size of the *Union List* has grown over the years and at present includes the holdings of some 40 college, special, and public libraries throughout West Virginia plus the 8 libraries that now make up the West Virginia University Libraries system.

The format of the *Union List* has changed somewhat since the first edition was published in 1962. Publication was made possible by photoduplicating the computer printout of the database and adding a spiral binding. By 1971, the publication had grown in size to the point where it had to be published in two volumes. And by 1978, three volumes were needed. To keep the publication in manageable form, a decision was made to photoduplicate two reduced pages per leaf. Since 1982, the *Union List* has been available in a hard bound edition, replacing the spiral bound editions of previous years.

In the beginning the *Union List* was distributed free of charge to libraries. However, in 1977, a charge of $15.00 for libraries that participated in the project and $20.00 for non-participating libraries was initiated to help defray increasing publication costs. Today the price has increased to $45.00 and $55.00 respectively for the annual edition.

Originally, only one edition of the *Union List* was printed—the statewide edition. During the 1970s, call numbers for serial titles in the West Virginia University Libraries system were added to the database. This permitted the West Virginia University Libraries to publish an "in-house" edition listing locations, titles, holdings, and call numbers (if used) for use within the University community.

Since 1974, the "successive title" format for listing title changes has been implemented. In this format a separate entry is made for each new title. An effort is being made to convert the "latest title" entries; however, many still remain under latest title with cross references to connect the various title changes.

SCOPE OF THE LIST

Some confusion has arisen during the past few years in the West Virginia University Libraries system as to the scope of the *Union List*. Although the initial concept that the *Union List* is not an end in itself still exists, many view the list as a substitute for the serial record. Although resorting to the *Union List* is still the first step in any bibliographical investigation, the card catalog or serial record still remains a more definitive source to consult. Originally, only scientific, technical, and social science serials that were of interest in the development of resource sharing in the region were included. Omitted from the *Union List* were titles that were usually considered part of a general reference collection and could be supplied through interlibrary loan. A trend to include more titles has developed during the past few years. Today some of the major titles normally considered general reference works are included. An effort is currently being made, subject to the discretion of the editor of the *Union List*, to list all titles that are reported. Only two or three of the major newspapers are included. The more important West Virginia governmental serials are also listed. A majority of United States' and United Nations agencies' annual reports, bulletins, proceedings, etc., are likewise being listed. In other words, almost all of the items being cataloged at West Virginia University or reported by cooperating libraries are currently being included in an effort to broaden the base of the *Union List*. Some titles may be included in the West Virginia University Libraries "in-house" edition but not in the statewide edition, since the titles may or may not be of particular interest to other libraries.

ONLINE UNION LIST

Traditionally, union lists of periodicals have appeared only in paper format. Computer technology, however, has provided the means for the creation and manipulation of databases containing serial location/holdings information. And the arrival of more sophisticated computer technology has permitted databases to be retrieved online instead of being printed in book format. Today one such database management system is SPIRES, the *S*tanford *P*ublic *I*nformation *R*etrieval *S*ystem. SPIRES allows for the creation, ownership, and management of a collection of data. The basis of any SPIRES application is the "SPIRES file," in which the data is stored. The *West Virginia Union List* database was reformatted and stored in such a SPIRES file, thereby allowing an increased number of ways to access and retrieve the data.

This data management system permits searching strategies by keyword, exact title, or truncated keyword, and also permits use of the Boolean logical operators "and," "or," and "not." One important SPIRES feature is the capability of ongoing maintenance, a capability that permits updates to be made to the database at any time. In addition, "read only" access to the online union list is available through WVNET (West Virginia Network for Educational Telecomputing)[5] to the entire West Virginia University community as well as to every college or university under the jurisdiction of the West Virginia Board of Regents that has an authorized CMS (Conversational Monitor System) account and follows the necessary protocol for accessing the online union list.

Titles in the online union list are indexed by keywords that appear in the "Title Proper," "Formerly," "Continued As," or "Cross Reference (XRef)" fields in the tape-loaded database. When a search is entered, all titles that contain search words in any of these fields (in any order) will be retrieved. The online union list software permits either a prompted mode or a command mode. The prompted mode is used on all public terminals available in the West Virginia University Libraries. The latest version of the union list software, which was installed on August 29, 1985, permits some additional subcommands. Available subcommands and their functions are:

..HELP — Displays the "HELP" menu.

..PROMPT — Invokes the prompted searching mode. (This mode is designed for users who are unfamiliar with either the union list or SPIRES commands. In prompted mode, the user types in as many words of a title as are known in response to the

"TITLE?" prompt. The system will then display all titles that match the keywords typed in by the user. The prompted mode is used on the public terminals at library sites.)

..COMMAND — Returns the user from the prompted mode to the command mode.

..SEARCH — Displays the search group menu.

..QUIT — Returns the user to the CMS environment.

A print option is also available to print offline the results of a search containing a large number of titles.

To maximize the retrieval possibilities of items, the *Union List* is under the authority control of the editor of the *West Virginia Union List*. The bringing of like items together is the responsibility of the data management system. Some problems in the retrieval of items have arisen since the existing *Union List* computer programs and input were not designed to be an online system. These difficulties are being corrected, if possible, as they are encountered.

Currently, 24,230 records for 25 of the participating college and university libraries have been added to the online union list, including those of all 8 of the West Virginia University Libraries. To eliminate the inputting separately of data into both the tape-loaded database for the printed edition and the online SPIRES file for the online union list, the systems analyst for the West Virginia University Libraries wrote the necessary computer programs to (1) access the tape-loaded printed list data (Figure A), (2) send the selected data to the CMS environment, and (3) update the SPIRES file for the online union list display (Figure B). The CMS operating system, a sophisticated timesharing system, permits either full screen or line-oriented editing. Thus, multiple line changes, such as insert, delete, move, and copy, are possible.

Eventually all of the holdings in the printed list edition will be loaded into the SPIRES file. Once this is done, the necessity of maintaining two databases will be eliminated. And the capability of printing a statewide union list or a selected libraries list from the

```
     LIBRARY JOURNAL
        AC    47-  1922-
        BB    75-  1950-
        BUW   51-  1926-
 --> CL    CURRENT
        CLC    1-  1876-
 --> M     85-  1960-
              (MICROFILM) 1-84   1876-1959
 --> ME    CURRENT 1 YEAR
        NK    85-96, 100-106  1960-1981
```

FIGURE A. Data as it appears in the printed statewide edition.

```
LIBRARY JOURNAL

     {XREF: L J. LIBRARY JOURNAL

LIBRARY  : WISE LIBRARY
REMARKS  : LAST TEN YEARS IN BOUND PERIODICALS ROOM
HOLDINGS : 85- 1960-
                  CALL NO.: Z671  .L7
           1-84 1876-1959
                  CALL NO.: MICRO-FILM 744

LIBRARY  : LEARNING RESOURCES CENTER, CHARLESTON
HOLDINGS : CURRENT

LIBRARY  : EVANSDALE LIBRARY
HOLDINGS : CURRENT 1 YEAR
                  CALL NO.: LIBRARIAN'S OFFICE - UNCAT
```

FIGURE B. Online union list display from "SPIRES File"

online system will be possible when appropriate printing programs are written to produce these offline products.

PaULS PARTICIPATION

In 1981, West Virginia University began reporting serials to PaULS (the Pennsylvania Union List of Serials), which is available through the OCLC Online System. The union listing component of OCLC allows union list groups to create, maintain, and display online summary holdings information for serials. A local data record (LDR) is attached to a bibliographic record for the serial for the purpose of reporting holdings.

An early policy decision was made to do all retrospective serials cataloging by updating the OCLC bibliographic record with relevant data pertaining to the original publication in hand as required by the Level 1 standards for OCLC inputting and by AAACR2. It was soon discovered that this decision was very time-consuming and would impede the smooth progress of procuring serial titles in machine-readable form. Therefore, a revised decision was reached, whereby only the LDR would be created following the guidelines in the *Pennsylvania Union List of Serials Procedures Manual* edited by Timothy J. Sperry (1982) and the OCLC union listing standards. This procedure will still attach the OCLC library symbol to the bibliographic record. Furthermore, the purchase of a snapshot tape from OCLC of LDRs also provides a copy of the corresponding bibliographic records.

West Virginia University Libraries report holdings statements for union listing in accordance with the American National Standards Institute's *Standards for Serial Holdings Statements at the Summary Level* (ANSI Z39.42-1980). In 1986, a decision was made to follow the exceptional entry of microform serials as stated in the OCLC *Serials Control: User Manual,* Appendix E.5-E.7. These union listing guidelines permit the recording of microform holdings on the same LDR containing the hard copy holdings and thereby display both formats in response to a single search.

At West Virginia University, serial titles are cataloged by the periodicals librarian. Reporting of all serial activity, including new, ceased, corrected, or withdrawn titles, is done on a Cataloging Serials Notification form, which is sent to designated units and persons in the library system, including the editor of the *Union List*. When updates are made to the printed list, a WVU Local Data Record – Union Listing Worksheet (Figure C) is completed to add, update, or cancel the LDR in the OCLC Online System. The editor has responsibility for selecting the most appropriate bibliographic record to which the LDR will be attached. The title, OCLC control number, call number, remarks (if needed), SCHD, and SIHD fields are added to each worksheet, and all worksheets are then given to a library technical assistant (LTA), who actually enters the LDRs in the online system. The LTA enters the LDRs, prints a copy of each LDR offline, and gives the printouts to the editor for revision. The process is similar in the retrospective conversion of serials. Presearching OCLC in order to locate all existing online bibliographic records is done by the LTA. These records in addition to any existing incomplete LDRs are printed offline. The editor then selects the appropriate record or does further searching. If an LDR already exists, needed corrections are made to the printout for inputting. A new LDR requires that a worksheet be completed. In either event, the LDRs are given to the LTA for inputting into the OCLC Online System.

The Wise Library is responsible for the inputting of LDRs for all of the West Virginia University Libraries except the Law Library and the Medical Center Library. Approximately 43% of the serial titles in the libraries are now in machine-readable form. As of April 1987, a total of 11,171 LDRs have been entered into the OCLC Online System. Limited staff and OCLC terminal time (2-3 hours per day) have kept the number of LDRs input rather low. The average number input per year is 1,800-2,000.

A LOOK TO THE FUTURE

A union list of serials has a multifaceted personality. To produce one takes the cooperation of many. There must be a financial commitment to the project, and agreements must exist concerning resource sharing, guidelines governing the display of bibliographic and holdings data, the actual means of producing the list, and, most

```
WVU LOCAL DATA RECORD - UNION LISTING WORKSHEET

Title _____
      _____

OCLC no: _____          ACTION
Hld Lib: _____
CLNO: _____     ☐ New
RMKS: _____     ☐ Update
                                  ☐ Delete
                                  ☐ On WYLBUR List

SCHD _____
     _____
     _____

SIHD _____
     _____
     _____
```

FIGURE C

importantly, ongoing maintenance.[6] Since no one library subscribes to or owns retrospective runs of all serials, a union list is the basic tool for resource sharing. A review of the literature indicates that union lists of serials will be a thing of the future as they have been a thing of the past.

Once all of the serials in the West Virginia University Libraries are in machine-readable form, a decision as to whether or not a printed union list is still necessary will have to be made. The so-called "in-house" printed edition has not been published since the online union list has been in existence; moreover, the statewide edition is being produced at present on a year-to-year review basis. OCLC offline products could provide a printed union list for many libraries or for one library. Cost will play an important part. As more libraries in West Virginia participate in some form of online union listing, the need for the statewide printed list diminishes. The situation will be reviewed in its entirety in two or three years' time. Many decisions concerning the look of the *Union List* in the future will depend upon the integrated library system chosen for the West Virginia University Libraries and the serials component within that system.

ENDNOTES

1. Michael M. Reynolds was the Assistant Director of Libraries at West Virginia University from 1957-1964.

2. Michael M. Reynolds, comp., *Scientific, Technical and Science Serials in the West Virginia University Libraries* (Morgantown: West Virginia University Library, 1962), p. iii.

3. The second edition was also revised by Michael M. Reynolds. The third edition was revised by Lorise Boger Topliffe and was still published under the same title as the first edition.

4. Lorise Boger Topliffe was Senior Reference Librarian at West Virginia University Library (1957-1964), Chief Reference Librarian (1965-1967), and Chief Bibliographer and Editor of the *West Virginia Union List* (1968-1971).

5. WVNET (West Virginia Network for Educational Telecomputing) serves the computing needs of the West Virginia Board of Regents system of higher education. WVNET supplies hardware and software computer resources to state-supported colleges and universities in West Virginia.

6. Marjorie E. Bloss. "Union Lists of Serials' Futures: Buy? Sell? or Keep What You've Got?" *Technical Services Quarterly*, 1 (Fall/Winter 1983): 159-170.

PaULS Participation by a Special Library

Betty P. Schwarz, MS, MLS

SUMMARY. Special librarians in Western Pennsylvania have long had an interest in resource sharing. Keeping union lists of serials current requires continuing cooperation. This article describes the procedures of the library of Calgon Corporation for updating its records in the new environment of online union lists.

Many special libraries in corporations are small, and have small budgets and very specific subject interests. These libraries may be very well equipped in their specialties but quite dependent on outside resources for answers to the many disparate questions that are asked. The ability to find answers and locate and obtain documents quickly and inexpensively is the hallmark of the staffs of the best of these libraries. The telephone, computer accessible databanks, a few directors, professional contacts, energy, and imagination are the tools of the trade.

These libraries need relationships with similar libraries in order to find specialized materials. They need relationships with geographically close libraries for convenience and ease of access. The relationships are formalized in such subject interest groups as the Chemistry Division, the Museum, Arts and Humanities Division, or the Military Librarians Division of the Special Libraries Associa-

---

Betty P. Schwarz is Manager, Information Center, Calgon Corporation, Box 1346, Pittsburgh, PA 15230. Mrs. Schwarz worked as a chemist prior to her career in information science. She has served as President of the Pittsburgh Chapter of the Special Libraries Association and Chairman of the Pittsburgh Chapter of the American Society for Information Science. She is currently a member of the PRLC Serials Management Committee and has served on the PaULS Advisory Committee.

tion (SLA). Geographic associations are also formed within local chapters of SLA and within library consortia such as the Pittsburgh Regional Library Center (PRLC).

Obtaining materials has become easier during the last decade than it was. The growth of online services has simplified the identification of materials. And document delivery services have made the materials accessible, as has the appearance of online union lists.

Computer access to union lists on OCLC has enhanced the ability of libraries to share resources regionally. Through the efforts of the State Library of Pennsylvania, PALINET, and PRLC, group access to OCLC interlibrary loan is available to libraries that do not otherwise participate in OCLC. The Pennsylvania Union List of Serials (PaULS) in its dynamic, online form is accessible to libraries that were formerly dependent on a microfiche version lacking the latest updates.

Printed union lists are expensive to produce, difficult to coordinate and maintain, and become outdated quickly. The history of *The Pittsburgh Regional Union List of Periodicals*, as found in the Foreword to the second edition, hints at the difficulties:

> Early in the 1920's the Pittsburgh Chapter of the Special Libraries Association undertook to identify periodical resources for the region. Printed editions of the file were issues by the chapter in 1926 and 1934; however, the problems of producing a traditional book catalog of an ever-increasing file of data discouraged additional printed editions under SLA auspices. By 1948, maintenance of the file of information on periodical holdings was being supported by the Carnegie Institute of Technology, the Carnegie Library of Pittsburgh, and the University of Pittsburgh, with service of the file being provided by the Science and Technology Department of the Carnegie Library of Pittsburgh.
>
> Conversion of the file to machine-readable form and the simplification of file maintenance were made possible by a grant from the State Library of Pennsylvania in 1967. The first edition produced from the computerized file appeared in 1970 as an "editorial" or working edition.
>
> The second edition incorporates corrections and updating of

that earlier volume. In addition, the holdings of a number of Libraries not previously participating in the *Union List* have been added. This work was also made possible by grants from the State Library of Pennsylvania in 1972 and 1973.[1]

The gap between editions—1934 until 1970, and 1973 until the appearance of PaULS in the early 1980s—underlines the problem.

Computer access to PaULS will allow member libraries to maintain their own records and thus spread the job throughout the system. The hope is that participating libraries will realize the value in keeping this resource alive. The appeal is to altruism, good citizenship, cooperation, and self-interest. After all, if Library A does not join, participate, and maintain its records, why should Library B, where all those things are done, honor requests from Library A?

Calgon participated in *The Pittsburgh Regional List of Periodicals*. We watched the volumes grow old and the data become unreliable. We received requests for material long gone from our collection. In 1981, Calgon became a voting member of PRLC and an OCLC participant. We were ready for PaULS and anxious to clear out our records. We had had enough telephone calls from people who, having found the *Regional List,* insisted that we had to have a journal because "This list says you have it."

Calgon's Information Center has a staff of two. For this reason many tasks are done in batches rather than as ongoing projects. When PaULS became a reality and OCLC began production of offline products, we chose to have a list of our serial holdings produced. Placing the first order was an adventure. There are many options available to tailor the list to a particular library's needs. These options are presented on the order form as a series of tags from a bibliographic record. To the uninitiated or only partially initiated person, this list of three-digit numbers is more than one ever wants to face (Figure 1). To find several such choices on one form could cause a change in careers. However, help was available from PRLC and from Ruth Carter of the University of Pittsburgh, then Chair of the PRLC Union List Committee. Having been told which boxes to check, we were not surprised to receive an excellent list of our serial holdings, as recorded in 1973.

The list sat admired but unused for many months because no one

SERIAL IDENTIFICATION AREA

DO YOU WANT ALL OPTIONS? ☐ yes ☐ no

If you want all options, do not make any selections below. If you want some serial-id tags but not all, then select the options you wish to include.

☐ 010	☐ 050	☐ 060	☐ 082	☐ 086	☐ 090	☐ 092	☐ 096
☐ 210	☐ 212	☐ 222	☐ 240	☐ 242	☐ 246	☐ 247	☐ 265
☐ 300	☐ 310	☐ 315	☐ 321	☐ 350	☐ 400	☐ 410	☐ 411
☐ 440	☐ 490	☐ 500	☐ 504	☐ 506	☐ 510	☐ 512	☐ 515
☐ 520	☐ 525	☐ 530	☐ 533	☐ 538	☐ 546	☐ 547	☐ 550
☐ 555	☐ 570	☐ 580	☐ 600	☐ 610	☐ 611	☐ 630	☐ 650
☐ 651	☐ 652	☐ 690 N/A	☐ 691 N/A	☐ 692 N/A	☐ 693 N/A	☐ 694 N/A	☐ 695 N/A
☐ 700	☐ 710	☐ 711	☐ 730	☐ 752	☐ 760	☐ 762	☐ 765
☐ 767	☐ 770	☐ 772	☐ 775	☐ 776	☐ 777	☐ 780	☐ 785
☐ 787	☐ 800	☐ 810	☐ 811	☐ 830	☐ 840		
☐ 100 (2nd ind. 1)		☐ 110 (2nd ind. 1)		☐ 111 (2nd ind. 1)			

FIGURE 1. A portion of the OCLC union list offline products order form.

was ready to tackle this new job. Finally, the inspiration came. OCLC would be producing another set of offline products and, if we learned to update our PaULS records, Calgon's new list would represent its current holdings.

The easiest and most enjoyable part of this process was the removal of 370 titles, reflecting the sale of a division of Calgon in the 1970s. The next task was the updating of our serial records. Our guide in doing this was *The Pennsylvania Union List of Serials Procedure Manual*,[2] edited by Timothy J. Sperry and published by PRLC in 1982. This manual describes procedures and contains samples and guidelines.

In this first attempt, many records were in need of editing. Our only difficulty came about as a result of poor communication. The person doing the updating was very experienced in using Interlibrary Loan on OCLC, but did no cataloging and had never entered a field delimiter, the character that separates subfields in a record. When accessing OCLC through a telephone and modem, known as "dial access," the field delimiter is a control code that appears as a "$" on the screen. One must know which keys on the terminal generate the control code. One cannot simply type a "$" and make the system work. However, there is no reason that a person would suspect this to be the case.

At first, the system would accept no data. Outside help from knowledgeable and friendly people was sought. A dedicated OCLC terminal was being used, and unfortunately the dial access problem was not solved until after many telephone calls had been placed and much hair-pulling had occurred. We were all embarrassed to have been perplexed by so small a detail. Once this obstacle was cleared, updating proceeded easily. Seventy-one (71) records were edited.

In order to update a PaULS entry, it is necessary to logon to OCLC using a serials control authorization number, enter "select" and a three-character institutional symbol, and then retrieve the OCLC local data record. After this, one looks at fields SCHD and SIHD and assesses one's holdings information (Figure 2). If one's holdings are incorrect, guidelines for correct headings can be found in the *PRLC Manual* in the section headed SCHD. Attention to these guidelines helps keep PaULS clean and useful. Finally, one edits the data and updates the record.

1. Sign-on to OCLC using your SERIALS CONTROL authorization number:

   nnn-nn-nnnscs+

   HELLO USER.
   You will be using the SERIALS CONTROL system in the FULL mode.

2. To retrieve only your own records, enter "select" and your institutional code (XXX) :

   select xxx\+

   You are using the SERIALS CONTROL System in the FULL mode. When you enter a bibliographic search key (with or without qualifiers), the system will retrieve only bibliographic records with 'XXX' attached.

3. Search for the desired title (if working from your printed holdings list, the OCLC number is known and is the best search key) :

   #2240427\+

   Modern paint and coatings.
   ISSN: 0098-7786   CODEN: MPCODM OCLC no: 2240427 Frequn: m Regulr: r

   Hld lib: XXXX Copy: Repr: Susc Stat: Loan:
   1 DEFN $v vol. $p no. $e 1 2 3 4 5 6 7 8 9 10 11 12 $f m $g [$p]
   2 SCHD $d 8603 $g 0 $e 4 $v 74- $y 1984-
   3 SIHD   PCA $d 8603 $g 0 $e 4 $v 74- $y 1984-

4. Change your data in fields SCHD and SIHD as required and update the record.

FIGURE 2. Updating a local data record.

Having edited Calgon's PaULS holdings, we could move on to entering the 60 titles for which we had no records in PaULS. The *PRLC Manual* again served as a guide for creating holdings statements. By this time, we were becoming experts.

In adding one's holdings to PaULS, one logs on to OCLC using a serials control authorization number. This is done by entering "select oluc," retrieving an appropriate bibliographic record, entering the command "wfc" to create a workform (Figure 3), entering one's data following the guidelines in the *PRLC Manual*, and updating one's record.

The result of this effort was that a professionally assembled, useful serials list (Figure 4) was produced for Calgon's use, and our

1. Sign-on to OCLC using your SERIALS CONTROL authorization number:

   nnn-nn-nnnscs+

   HELLO USER.
   You will be using the SERIALS CONTROL system in the FULL mode.

2. To retrieve any record, enter "select oluc":

   select oluc\+

   You are using the SERIALS CONTROL System in the FULL mode. When you enter a bibliographic search key (with or without qualifiers), the system will retrieve all bibliographic records matching your search key in the Online Union Catalog.

3. Search for the serial record:

   jou,of,in,d/ser\+
      Screen 1 of 2
         1 Journal of Indian dance   L'Institut de Kathali de Montrèal
   =Montreal Institute of Kathali, 1982 s NLC
         2...

         11 Journal of investigative dermatology   Williams & Wilkins.
   1938 s DLC
         12 Journal of investigative dermatology   Appleton-Century-Crofts
   [etc.] 1960 s NLM

4. Select the desired record:

   11\+
      Screen 1 of 3
      NO HOLDINGS IN PCA - FOR HOLDINGS ENTER dh DEPRESS DISPLAY
      RECD SEND
      OCLC; 988051   Rec stat: c Entrd: 740823   Used: 870407
      Type:

      14 049   PCAA
      15 210 0   J. invest. dermatol.

5. Create a workform by entering "wfc":

   wfc\+
   The Journal of investigative dermatology.
   ISSN: 0022-202X CODEN: JIDEAE OCLC no: 988051 Frequn: m Regulr: r

      Hld lib: PCAA Copy: Repr: Subsc Stat: Loan:

      1 CLNO $b
      2 LOCN $b
      3...

6. Enter data and update the record.

FIGURE 3. Entering holdings in PaULS.

CALGON CORPORATION - SERIALS LIST

Mineral processing & extracting metallurgy
   See:
   Transactions. Section C. Mineral processing &
   extractive metallurgy / Institute of Mining
   & Metallurgy.

Minerals & materials. Washington, D.C. : U.S.
   Dept. of the Interior. Bureau of Mines.
   OCLC 2670505 : ISSN 0363 - 9622.
   PCA (retains latest 5 years)

Modern paint and coatings. Atlanta, etc.,
   Palmerton Pub. Co.
   v. 65- Jan. 1975-
   OCLC2240427 : ISSN :0098-7786:CODEN MPCODM
   Continues: PVP. Paint and varnish production
   PCA 74- 1984-

Modern Plastics. New York, N.Y. : McGraw-Hill
   OCLC 4696134 : ISSN 0026-8275:CODEN MOPLAY
   Continues: Plastic products
   PCA (CURRENT 5 YEARS)

FIGURE 4. Sample entry from Calgon's union list offline product.

records were up-to-date for others to use. Since we had received excellent guidance when ordering our initial list and had been satisfied with the product, there was no need to change the specifications.

We elected to receive another serials holdings list in 1987. Once again, PaULS holdings were edited before production. This was a much easier task since it reflected only the current year's changes.

We expect to continue this process at Calgon, as it fits neatly into our serials control scheme. Renewal decisions are made in early autumn for December expiration dates. The results of these decisions are recorded in our PaULS entries in late winter. The serials holdings list is received in the spring.

This practice keeps PaULS current, enhancing its usefulness to everyone. Calgon benefits from having the holdings list, from not receiving requests for material not held, and from having PaULS to use.

NOTES

1. *Pittsburgh Regional Union List of Periodicals*, second edition. Pittsburgh: Pittsburgh Regional Library Center, Inc., 1973, p. III.
2. Timothy J. Sperry, ed., *Pennsylvania Union List of Serial Procedures Manual*. [Pittsburgh]: Pittsburgh Regional Library Center, 1982, 30 p.

Serial Union Listing in a Regional Academic Consortium

Susan A. Cady, MLS, MPA

SUMMARY. The transition from an IBM punch card-based regional union list of serials to an OCLC-based union listing system is described. The Lehigh Valley Association of Independent Colleges (LVAIC), a cooperative of six private colleges in eastern Pennsylvania, dealt with issues of scope, funding, conversion contract language and administration, and bibliographic policy. Concerns are raised about patrons' ability to use easily the printed list produced by OCLC. However, the list is too new to be evaluated yet in terms of format, scope, cost, or quality.

THE LEHIGH VALLEY ASSOCIATION OF INDEPENDENT COLLEGES

The Lehigh Valley Association of Independent Colleges (LVAIC) was established in 1969 to promote cooperative action, expand educational opportunities, and achieve greater efficiency and economy among the five private colleges and single university located in the greater Allentown/Bethlehem/Easton area of eastern Pennsylvania. The institutions that belong to the Association are:

Allentown College of St. Francis De Sales, Center Valley
Cedar Crest College, Allentown
Lafayette College, Easton

Susan A. Cady is Associate Director for Technical Services at Lehigh University Libraries, Bethlehem, PA 18015. Mrs. Cady has been active in the area of library cooperation since 1972. She has recently served as President of PALINET.

Lehigh University, Bethlehem
Moravian College, Bethlehem
Muhlenberg College, Allentown

Together these schools serve a constituency of more than 14,000 students, 1,000 teaching faculty, and 700 administrative and support personnel. With a population of approximately 650,000, the Lehigh Valley is the third largest metropolitan area in Pennsylvania.

From its inception, library cooperation has been one of the Association's most successful endeavors. In fact, the libraries' cooperative activities preceded the formal establishment of LVAIC by several years. Cooperative programs relating to libraries include, but are not limited to:

- union list of serials
- union mediography
- investigation of shared local systems
- reciprocal borrowing
- joint statement on copyright
- shared consultants
- cooperative collection development
- regular meetings of directors and other staff groups
- daily inter-institutional delivery service
- group participation in the Interlibrary Delivery Service of Pennsylvania

Many additional cooperative programs have been developed by the consortium, such as cross-registration, summer study abroad, academic lecture series, a shared travel agency, and group purchasing.

INITIATION OF THE LVAIC UNION LIST

In the late 1960s the LVAIC library directors decided they would like to initiate an automated union list of current periodicals, similar to those developed at Lehigh University for the Mart Science and Engineering and Linderman Libraries. These early lists, which were produced on computers at Lehigh University, were essentially printouts of IBM keypunch cards manually arranged in alphabetic order.

Lehigh's Technical Coordinator for Serials, Kenneth Veprek, served as editor of the new list, which was updated semiannually. The *LVAIC Union List of Periodicals* contained a summary holdings statement only for the institution which owned the longest run of a given periodical. The list indicated that some lesser amount of holdings was also present at other institutions by way of symbols for those institutions but did not give specific holdings.

THE UNION LIST OF SERIALS

In the late 1970s it was decided to expand and improve the *LVAIC Union List of Periodicals*. When it appeared in early 1979, the 580-page new edition included the following features:

1. An expanded definition of serials to include annual and irregular publications. Proceedings, advances, and annual reviews were thus included.
2. Identification of each library's holdings. As mentioned above, the first generation of the list cited the longest run only. Other libraries with holdings were identified without holdings information.
3. Discontinued and ceased publications. The previous edition was restricted to active subscriptions.

This phase also encompassed improvements in production with a true (COBOL) computer program written by Lehigh University Administrative Systems programmers. The data was now stored on magnetic tape with keypunch cards used for updates. At the same time, an expanded organizational structure supported the production of the list with an LVAIC Serials Committee, composed of representatives from each of the participating institutions, working together on the list. At least one of the planned annual updates to this edition of the list was completed before the quickening pace of library automation pulled LVAIC into the next generation of union listing technology.

THE DECISION TO CONVERT
TO OCLC UNION LISTING

Even as the LVAIC academic institutions were busy with production of their expanded and improved union list, OCLC Inc., the nation's largest bibliographic utility, was bringing into operation its new online union listing capability. In late 1979 an OCLC-based statewide union list of serials was initiated. The *Pennsylvania Union List of Serials* or PaULS, as it came to be known, was funded by Title III of the *Library Services and Construction Act* and directed by the Pittsburgh Regional Library Center under contract to the State Library of Pennsylvania.[1] Lehigh, Lafayette, Cedar Crest, and Muhlenberg participated in one or more phases of the construction of this list, which began with approximately 2,000 core titles and a controlled number of institutions. Lehigh's Serials Coordinator, Kenneth Veprek, served as a member of the PaULS Advisory Committee.

At least three circumstances led to the decision to convert the LVAIC List to the OCLC union listing facility. Several institutions began to be overwhelmed by the sheer volume of serial list activities, combined with numerous in-house automated cataloging priorities in preparation for local systems. For instance, the Lehigh University Libraries, which had the largest number of holdings to contribute to the LVAIC list and had taken a leadership role in its production under Kenneth Veprek, had never abandoned its own two keypunch card-based serial lists tailored to the needs of the Mart Science and Engineering Library and the Linderman Library, and now found itself involved in the production of three separate serial lists. At the same time all members of the Association were becoming interested in obtaining machine-readable records for their serial titles. Finally, the batch production method and the computer programs that created the union list were both in need of modernization, given changes taking place in Lehigh University computing facilities.

A glimmer of light appeared at the end of this serials tunnel when it was learned that the State Library of Pennsylvania had begun awarding *Library Services and Construction Act* funds to regional union list groups around the state to assist them in conversion of their lists to the OCLC system and thereby enriching the PaULS database. (See Appendix A for a complete list of such projects funded to date by the State Library of Pennsylvania.) The LVAIC libraries were in agreement that outside help was an absolute necessity in order to make the transition, and welcomed the idea of outside contracting as well as outside funding. It is a familiar irony that almost all advances in both service and efficiency in libraries seem to require enormously labor-intensive conversion operations that limited staffs coping with day to day tasks cannot add to their workloads. Even in production of the 1979 serial list, the LVAIC budget had supported some assistance through funding of keypuncher positions and some other costs. Thus in May 1984 a grant proposal was submitted to the State Library of Pennsylvania requesting LSCA funds for the conversion of the *LVAIC Union List of Serials* to the OCLC system. The approved budget, which totalled $45,511, included funds for a conversion contract, profiling, training, first year storage of local data records, initial offline product costs, and various other miscellaneous items.

FROM IDEA TO IMPLEMENTATION

Notification of the award of these funds in July 1984 allowed LVAIC to begin working in earnest on the many tasks associated with the implementation. Even contracted conversions require much work on the part of the participating institutions. The first task was to choose a contractor for the project. RFPs were submitted to OCLC Inc., PALINET, and PRLC. In July 1985, a contract was signed with PRLC, the lowest bidder and the contractor for the original *Pennsylvania Union List of Serials.*

The LVAIC Serials Committee, composed of serials and/or cataloging librarians at the member institutions, took responsibility for making many decisions that guided the contractor's day to day operations on the conversion project. Kenneth Veprek served as technical liaison with PRLC. The Serials Committee members are listed in Appendix B. Some of the most important issues and their resolution are outlined below.

One issue was the definition of the scope of the project since the funds awarded did not appear to be sufficient to convert the entire list. As a result, any original cataloging as well as certain categories of materials were excluded, such as series, etc. Furthermore, it was decided not to convert any serial for which a successive entry record could not be found in the OCLC database.

The issue of how to treat microform holdings arose, as it does in the case of many lists. Up to that time, LVAIC libraries participating in PaULS had followed AACR2 practice with the creation of a separate bibliographic record for microform holdings. At Lehigh various notes had been added to the local data records so that users could see the entire holdings on one local data record, usually the record for the printed version of the serial. This approach was abandoned in the LVAIC Union List project as it has been more recently in a number of other projects, including the OCLC-based United States Newspaper Program.[2] All holdings, including microform, are posted on the record for the paper copy.

It was also decided that the Lehigh University titles should be converted first since they were the most numerous and had already been converted to successive entry form to a larger extent than had other member holdings. The Committee was particularly concerned that all member holdings of a given title be attached to the same record, a goal that might seem easy to achieve to those not familiar with the intricacies of serials and the OCLC database. The direction to convert the Lehigh titles first did, however, present a problem to the contractor because this subset had the most obscure and difficult serials in it and did not allow for the best workflow at the contractor's office.

Another major issue in the conversion was the definition of quality control standards and the methodology to be used in testing for the agreed-upon quality. Although the contract specified that quality control standards had to be met by the contractor, it further stated that the standards and methodology for testing would be negotiated between PRLC and LVAIC at a later date. This proved to be a difficult task, and it delayed implementation somewhat. Naturally the libraries wanted the best possible product, and the contractor wished to produce a good product too, but one which would not be done at a loss. A change in the Executive Director at PRLC further added to delays. A partial excerpt from the final quality control agreement is reproduced in Appendix C.

PRODUCTION AND USE OF THE LVAIC LIST

The conversion of the list began in earnest in late 1985 and was completed in early 1987, in advance of the May 1987 production of the offline printed product. The first copies were duplicated in early June 1987 as a four volume set and given limited distribution since the LVAIC Serials Committee felt that the first printed list should serve as a draft list that would allow for the making of corrections and refinements.

At the time of the decision to convert the LVAIC union list to OCLC, a study had been done to estimate the number of titles and holdings for each institution. A comparison of the statistical profile from that study and the first OCLC produced offline product is given below:

	OCLC LIST	LOCAL LIST
pages	2263	648
unique titles	19771	20777
total holdings	28050	28739

More than 7,200 OCLC local data records had been created by Cedar Crest, Lafayette, Lehigh, and Muhlenberg before the start of the project by virtue of their participation in the PaULS list and Lehigh's participation in the OCLC serial control subsystem. It was expected that the number of holdings statements would increase in the OCLC-based list by approximately 25% as a result of normal growth (the last local list was dated 1983) and of title splits necessitated by successive entry cataloging since the LVAIC list of serials had included both latest and successive entry cataloging. However, it was after these calculations that the decision was made to eliminate original cataloging and to exclude some categories of serials in order to conserve funds. Although the numbers of local holdings statements are very similar, no doubt there are differences in the actual titles included.

Use of the LVAIC List has always been heavy, both by reference staff and patrons in the member libraries. At the author's institution, both patrons and staff use the list daily. Interlibrary loan staff rely heavily on the online version of the list. There is concern that the printed format of the OCLC-based list will be difficult for patrons to use because of the abundance of bibliographic information and the designation of locations by 049 codes rather than by more familiar abbreviations.

THE NEXT GENERATION

The immediate priority for the LVAIC Serials Committee is the clean-up and refinement of the product delivered by the contractor and OCLC, as suggested above. Yet there are already other interesting possibilities on the horizon. These possibilities take advantage of the existence of a standardized group list available on magnetic tape that can be manipulated in a variety of ways. It must be pointed out, however, that since the author of this article is associated with Lehigh University and such matters have not been formally raised at LVAIC meetings, they represent only the thoughts of one interested party at one institution.

The improvements suggested below fall into two categories: producing a customized printed product from the magnetic tape version of the list and loading holdings information directly into a local online system from the tape. At the Lehigh University Libraries the reference staff have had a number of reservations about the OCLC printed union list product which has been in use as an institutional list for at least three years. As mentioned above, the amount and complexity of bibliographic information included in the printed list are felt to be confusing to undergraduate students, who are interested primarily in the location of the serial, i.e., the building (Fairchild-Martindale or Linderman Library) and the call number. The building location must be inferred from an obscure OCLC 049 code and the call number is not highlighted in any way. Figure 1 illustrates this problem by exhibiting the same record as it appears in both the locally produced old LVAIC list and the OCLC list. If a union list magnetic tape was purchased by the consortia instead of the printed product, all members of the union list could probably save money on printed serial lists for their own institutions and enjoy some degree of customization. Purchase of both union list group and institutional printed products results in double payment for the same records.

```
LOCALLY-PRODUCED LVAIC              OCLC-PRODUCED LVAIC
UNION LIST OF SERIALS               UNION LIST OF SERIALS


HARVARD ADVOCATE                    Harvard advocate. Cambridge, Mass. : Harvard
    LL    v.103,1969-                   Advocate.
                                        Began publication in 1869.
HARVARD BULLETINS IN EDUCATION          OCLC 8158155;ISSN 0017-8004
    LL    v.4,13-15,19,1917-37          Continues: Advocate (Cambridge, Mass.)
                                    LYU 103-  1969-
HARVARD BUSINESS REPORTS            LYUS  805 H339 103-  1969-
    MO    v.6,1928
    LL    v.1-11,1925-32            Harvard bulletins in education. Cambridge, Mass.
    LF    1925,1927,1930                : Harvard University. 1917-
                                        No. 4-
HARVARD BUSINESS REVIEW                 OCLC  1832206.
    MU    v.15,1936-                    Continues: Harvard-Newton bulletins
    MO    v.24,1946-               LYU 4, 13-15, 19  1917-1937
    LL    v.1,1922-                LYUM 370.6 H33b 4, 13-15, 19  1917-1937
    LF    v.1,1922-
    CC    v.40,1962-               Harvard business reports. Chicago, Ill. :
    AC    v.36,1958-                   Compiled and published for the Graduate School
                                       of Business Administration, George F. Baker
                                       Foundation, Harvard University [by] A. W. Shaw
                                       Company, 1925-1932.
                                       Vol. 1-11.
                                       OCLC  1638940.
                                   LYU 1-11  1925-1932
                                   LYUM 658 H33r  1-11  1925-1932

                                   Harvard business review. Boston [etc.] Graduate
                                       School of Business Administration, Harvard
                                       University.
                                       v.1-  Oct. 1922-
                                       OCLC  1751795;ISSN 0017-8012;CODEN HABRAX.
                                   ALL  36-  1958- (Microfilm:v.36,37,44-54, 1958-
                                       1976)
                                   ALLE 36-  1958- (Microfilm:v.36,37,44-54, 1958-
                                       1976)
                                   EVI  15-37,39-  1936-  (Current year at
                                       circulation desk.)
                                   EVII 15-37, 39-  1936-  (Current year at
                                       circulation desk.)
                                   EVIM 41-  1963-
                                   LAF  1-  1922-
                                       LAFA  658.05 H33 1-  1922-
                                   LYU  1-  1922-
                                       LYUY  658.05 H33br 1-  1922-
                                   MOR  25-  1946-
                                   MORA 25-  1946-
```

FIGURE I

Another future phase of the serial list might be the loading of the holdings information into local systems. Automation vendors can reformat the magnetic tapes so that they can be loaded into local systems with summary serial holdings intact. The GEAC system provides for display of summary holdings through a GEAC defined 930 tag. This might suggest that there is no need for a printed product at all; however, the ability to qualify searches by format in the GEAC system and (perhaps) some local trade-offs in indexing will be necessary before the average undergraduate can locate journal titles without having to sort through a bewildering number of initial search results.

CONCLUSION

To some extent the jury is still out on the success of the conversion of the LVAIC list to the OCLC union listing system from a local institution and regional consortium perspective. In addition to the previously described issue of end-user satisfaction, the issues of local updating responsibilities and continuing costs need to be considered in an overall evaluation. As Carter suggests in reference to the PaULS list,[3] maintenance of a list is more difficult than getting it started. A transition from the special project orientation to making update on an ongoing basis to the online list will be necessary. It is to be hoped that this will be welcomed by member libraries as a simple method of updating PaULS, the LVAIC union list, and local institutional lists simultaneously.

Cost is another important factor. Many costs are incurred along the way including those of LDR creation, LDR update, LDR storage, offline production, and duplication. Most of these costs are outside LVAIC's control. However, at a minimum the new list enables LVAIC and its members to obtain bibliographic and holdings data in standard format on magnetic tape so that the transition to the product of the next generation will be less labor-intensive and costly.

NOTES

1. Ruth C. Carter and Scott Bruntjen, "The Pennsylvania Union List of Serials: Initial Development," *The Serials Librarian* v.5 no.3 (Spring 1981):57-64.

2. Robert B. Harriman, Jr. "Coordination of Cataloging Practices in the United States Newspaper Program," *Cataloging & Classification Quarterly* v. 6 no. 4 (Summer 1986):15-29.

3. Ruth C. Carter and Scott Bruntjen, "The Pennsylvania Union List of Serials: From Development to Maintenance," *The Serials Librarian* v.8 no.4 (Summer 1984):55-67.

APPENDIX A
PENNSYLVANIA CONSORTIA FUNDED FOR CONVERSION TO OCLC UNION LISTING BY LSCA TITLE III

Associated College Libraries of Central Pennsylvania
Lehigh Valley Association of Independent Colleges
Health Information Libraries of Northeast Pennsylvania and Northeast Pennsylvania Bibliographic Center jointly
Northwest Interlibrary Cooperative of Pennsylvania
Pennsylvania Community College Library Consortia
Susquehanna Library Cooperative
Tri-State College Library Cooperative

APPENDIX B
LVAIC SERIALS COMMITTEE

Rita Berk, Moravian College
Dianne Melnychek, Cedar Crest/Muhlenberg Colleges
Kenneth Veprek, Lehigh University
Jacob Welle, Allentown College
Sharon Wiles-Young, Lafayette College

APPENDIX C
QUALITY CONTROL STANDARDS IN THE LVAIC CONVERSION

SAMPLE SELECTION

Every 10th record to which an individual library in LVAIC has its holdings attached will constitute the test sample. If the same record is selected for two or more libraries using this methodology that record will be evaluated twice just as if it had been chosen twice through random number selection. Any record for which the holding library failed to respond to a PRLC report/question form will be eliminated from the test sample.

Errors fall into two categories for the purposes of this test:

1. Incorrect Record Selection—either no record was selected when one should have been or an incorrect record was selected.
2. All Other Errors—any error other than incorrect record selection, including typographical errors.

ERROR TABULATION AND WEIGHTING

Each record shall have a potential of 0 to 2 errors, to be assigned as follows:

No errors in category 1 or 2	0
Category 1 errors only	2
Category 1 and category 2 errors	2
Category 2 error(s) only	1

To obtain the percentage of error the cumulative number of errors will be divided by twice the sample size and multiplied by 100. For example, a total sample of 3,000 with total error points of 300 yields an error rate of 5%.

PaULS:
A View from the Network

Rian Miller-McIrvine, MM, MLS

SUMMARY. The Pennsylvania Union List of Serials (PaULS) is an important resource sharing tool for libraries throughout the Commonwealth. One of the earliest union list projects undertaken utilizing a shared bibliographic database and adhering to emerging national standards, PaULS served as a model for several OCLC-based statewide union list projects undertaken during the last decade. Following a successful development period, the project experienced a number of difficulties in managing the transition from centralized data entry to decentralized maintenance. This paper discusses typical problems, outlines findings and insights gained during the project in the context of a more recent statewide union list project, and provides a prognosis for the future of the PaULS project.

I. THE EARLY STAGES: PLANNING AND DEVELOPMENT

Introduction

Union listing has long been recognized as an important component in an effective information delivery system. However, early attempts to create comprehensive and timely locator tools for serials were often unsuccessful. Lack of efficient mechanisms and adequate funds to update and disseminate printed or microform lists, coupled with the absence of widely accepted reporting standards, resulted in union lists that were often out-of-date, even upon publication, and frequently difficult to use.

In the mid-1970s, several important trends came together, and in

---

Rian Miller-McIrvine is Manager, OCLC Services Division, PALINET, 3401 Market Street, Suite 262, Philadelphia, PA 19104.

doing so provided an impetus to create online interactive union lists in a network environment. The availability of relatively affordable "real-time" computer power for library applications and the emergence of OCLC as a prototype for a national shared database established strong underpinnings for automation initiatives and resource sharing. The inauguration of the CONSER Project, consensus on the necessity of a uniform method of reporting serial holdings data, and the failed attempt to create a national periodicals center highlighted the need to develop an effective means for disseminating bibliographic as well as holdings information.

The purpose of this article is to review the development of the Pennsylvania Union List of Serials (PaULS) from the perspective of a regional network, to identify problems associated with the creation and maintenance of large union lists, and to discuss difficulties encountered in the transition from centralized data entry to decentralized maintenance. Knowledge gained from the project and a prognosis concerning the future of the PaULS database are also discussed.

PaULS: Planning and Development from the Network Perspective

Efforts to develop an online union list for Pennsylvania libraries began as early as 1974, and have been documented by Carter and Bruntjen.[1,2,3] A widely available statewide union list based on nationally accepted standards was viewed as an important tool for promoting resource sharing, especially among libraries in the Commonwealth. In addition to providing easy access to serial holdings, it was also perceived that a comprehensive union list would serve to distribute borrowing and lending activities more evenly.

From a network perspective, PaULS was an important project. Creation of a statewide union list would enhance PALINET's ability to fulfill its fundamental mission of advancing resource sharing through automation. PALINET, a network serving libraries in eastern and central Pennsylvania, New Jersey, Delaware, and Maryland, has a long history of promoting library cooperation. Since the inception of the Union Library Catalogue of Pennsylvania in 1935, the network has been providing location and referral services for libraries throughout the Commonwealth for over 50 years. Support for automation initiatives in libraries has been the primary thrust of the network's service program for the past fifteen years.

Clearly, PaULS was a project with potential benefits for all types and sizes of libraries. In addition to its being an online interactive union list, PaULS held the promise of stimulating library cooperation, while also providing individual libraries with the opportunity to automate serial holdings data. It was recognized from the outset, however, that to be successful PaULS had to offer tangible results — specifically easy access to up-to-date holdings information.

The PaULS project represented one of the earliest attempts to create a multi-institutional, comprehensive union list using a shared bibliographic database and adhering closely to national standards. To a large extent, PaULS has set the standard for many OCLC-based statewide union list projects undertaken during the past decade. From the network viewpoint, the project required planning in the absence of clear precedent, implementation of a database with limited source records of serial publications, policy formation amidst the evolution of standards as well as technology, and lobbying to forge new relationships among libraries sometimes not yet convinced of the benefits of automation.

The creation of the PaULS database called for a two-step approach. Early in the development phase, the Pittsburgh Regional Library Center (PRLC), in cooperation with the University of Pittsburgh, completed an agreement with OCLC to tapeload bibliographic and holdings data from pre-existing machine-readable union list files. The data, including holdings for libraries in western Pennsylvania, represented a significant enhancement to the Online Union Catalog maintained by OCLC. Once tapeloading was completed, centralized data entry of a core list of titles held by selected libraries was initiated.[4]

Upon completion of the original database, it was anticipated that maintenance would be assumed by libraries contributing to the union list. Supported by LCSA funds provided by the State Library of Pennsylvania, centralized inputting continued over a period of six years. By September 1983 PaULS contained over 60,000 titles.

While the model for database creation was sound, the implementation cycle required longer than anticipated. As the final year of centralized input drew to a close, plans were made to transfer maintenance activity to individual union list participants. Staff members of the networks and the State Library met to develop a framework for decentralized maintenance. PALINET staff approached this stage of the project with considerable apprehension about the long-term viability of PaULS, given finite funding. Experience with other resource sharing initiatives suggested that local priorities would naturally take precedence over statewide projects unless the benefits of cooperation were obvious and compelling.

The plan for decentralization assigned to PRLC continuing responsibility for such matters as maintaining the group profile, scheduling production of offline products, and providing and/or securing updating services for non-OCLC union list participants. The University of Pittsburgh continued to serve as a source of expertise in matters of bibliographic quality control and interpretation of holdings standards. Overall direction of the project rested with the State Library of Pennsylvania's Library Development Division. Training responsibility was assigned to PALINET and PRLC. Development, review, and distribution of a PaULS procedure manual was a joint endeavor by the networks.

II. FROM CENTRALIZED CREATION TO DECENTRALIZED MAINTENANCE: MANAGING THE TRANSITION

The transition to decentralized maintenance of the PaULS database was not an easy one. Many years had intervened since libraries were queried for holdings data. With inevitable staff turnover and changes in libraries' priorities, interest in PaULS had flagged considerably by the close of 1983.[5] The momentum needed to propel the distributed maintenance effort had been dissipated.

Problems related to maintenance of holdings for non-OCLC members of PaULS remained unresolved, and consensus was not achieved on issues of bibliographic control and quality assurance. Delays in union listing development occurred at OCLC, and uncertainties regarding continued funding for the project also hindered efforts to decentralize maintenance activities.

In addition, difficulties and delays in generating offline products for wide distribution caused many libraries to dismiss PaULS as a locator tool, especially in institutions without online access to OCLC. Production of a COM version of the union list had been established as one of the requirements of the PaULS project. While beyond the control of PaULS project staff, the failure to provide ready access to holdings data for the entire population of union list participants hampered efforts to encourage local updating.

Problems associated with the post-conversion period of the PaULS project appear to typify large union lists. Efforts to manage such projects and to promote data maintenance present many challenges. For purposes of discussion, planning and maintenance issues can be divided into six broad categories: (1) administrative; (2) organizational; (3) technical; (4) financial; (5) instructional; and (6) motivational.

Administrative and Organizational Issues

The transition from centralized input to decentralized maintenance raises a number of substantial administrative issues. Specifically, large union list groups require mechanisms for monitoring quality control, recommending and administering policies, communicating policy decisions and other information to group members, educating library staff regarding maintenance requirements, promoting the union list, and recruiting new participants.

An issue of primary importance in any union list project is consistent quality control over both bibliographic record selection and data entry. The value of any union list hinges on collection of holdings data with a single bibliographic description. Only one look-up should be required to determine all holding locations. Assigning responsibility for record selection and bibliographic quality control to one or more agencies is an administrative task that cannot be ignored. Such a responsibility cannot be random or uncertain in the way in which it is carried out.

As the plan to decentralize PaULS was developed, continued centralized control of bibliographic activities was recommended. Unfortunately, this recommendation was not implemented. To a certain extent, union list projects undertaken currently face fewer obstacles in the area of quality control. The Online Union Catalog has reached a consistent level of stability, and quality control efforts continue to enjoy a high corporate priority at OCLC. In addition, relatively recent enhancements to OCLC's union listing capability make it possible to identify readily bibliographic records already in use by other members of the specific union list group. However, a large union list group should consider carefully the range of activities associated with ensuring quality control and both appoint and fund one or more agencies to oversee these activities.

Essential to the long-term success of a large union list is a well-organized advisory committee charged with recommending and administering policy. Ideally, members of the committee should be firmly committed to the union list idea and knowledgeable about the resource sharing goals of the group. As changes occur in cataloging rules and holdings standards, as well as in practices observed by bibliographic utilities, union list groups must be prepared to evaluate and control the impact on maintenance activities. Other issues that must be addressed at an advisory group level are scope of the list both in terms of participants and types of materials to be included, maintenance for participants that may not have online access to the database, selection or rejection of options provided for representing holdings data, frequency and formats of offline products, and sources of funding for union list support.

The PaULS structure provided for a ten member advisory committee charged with monitoring activities of the union list group. Consisting of eight librarians and two members representing national interests, the committee met frequently in the early stages of the project. However, as centralized activity drew to a close and continued funding became uncertain, the emergence of divergent priorities caused a fracturing of the committee process. This experience underscores the importance of consensus building as well as compromise among committee members charged with charting the course for a union list group.

Promoting the union list and recruiting new members are administrative concerns often overlooked. To remain vital, a union list must be perceived as a useful tool, one worthy of the effort required to maintain it. New members should continue to be sought in an effort to enhance the list through increased holdings and locations. Promotion techniques should focus on the value and effectiveness of the union list in satisfying local needs and in expediting efficient document delivery. Inextricably linked to promotion is communication of information about the union list and its benefits to participants.

Educating library staff about union listing can be a formidable task. Starting at the top, administrators must not only be convinced of the value of the union list, they must also be persuaded to allocate adequate resources to support maintenance activities. Technical services staff must be thoroughly trained to access and update union list data. In some cases, recommendations must be made regarding changes in workflow to accommodate maintenance activities. Public services staff need to be trained to use the union list as a primary locator tool and, if appropriate, to update holdings data.

Organizational structures in libraries may hamper the educational process. Typically, technical services staff are charged with maintaining holdings data, but realize no direct benefit from updating activity. Conversely, public services staff derive direct benefit from access to current holdings data but are generally not involved in the maintenance process. To complicate the issue, it is not uncommon to encounter technical services units where serials staff do not have access to the online database in which the holdings are maintained. Therefore, when a change to holdings data is discovered by serials personnel, it is often not communicated to the staff responsible for managing the institution's bibliographic and holdings file online. Relationships among functional units within the library must be examined to ensure agreement on responsibilities for union list activities and availability of both resources and training opportunities.

From PALINET's perspective, bridging the gap between the technical and public services perspectives on the union list was an important goal in stimulating maintenance efforts. To work toward this end, the network sponsored a series of workshops during 1985 designed to encourage cooperative maintenance. Each workshop was divided into two half-day sections. The first section, presented to all attendees, stressed the importance of the PaULS project in the context of statewide resource sharing initiatives as well as the benefits of participation for individual libraries. An overview of OCLC's union list component was provided, and procedures for integrating maintenance activities into normal routines were recommended. During the second section, attendees were divided into two groups. Technical services staff received instruction in the basics of bibliographic record selection and holdings maintenance and completed a series of editing and updating exercises. Public services staff concentrated on learning to access and interpret union list data as a means of verifying holdings, and completed a series of searching exercises. The overall reaction to the workshop series was positive.

To summarize the administrative and organizational issues, union listing requires an effective advisory committee, consensus on the goals of the project, a plan for controlling and monitoring project activity, and the commitment and cooperation of several functional units within participating institutions. Leadership must be exercised to identify potential problems and seek appropriate solutions. Union list participants should be actively involved in establishing priorities, and must be kept informed of project progress.

Technical Issues

Technical issues associated with maintenance of a union list are many and varied. As noted earlier, record selection poses difficulty in a distributed environment. The inherent changeability of serials, the complexity of serials cataloging, and the need to understand and observe conventions of national projects such as CONSER combine to create a veritable "bibliographic jungle." Maintenance of PaULS on the OCLC system provides a rich case study for examining the difficulty of record selection in a decentralized mode. For many years, OCLC instructed union list participants to use only successive entry records for union listing. However, the Online Catalog contains many latest entry records created under earlier cataloging codes or according to standards peculiar to the Library of Congress (LC). Lacking adequate training in serials cataloging conventions, searchers are sometimes unable to differentiate between successive and latest entry cataloging. In cases where record selection is incorrect, holdings statements become linked to inappropriate bibliographic descriptions. In a union list environment, the problem of incorrect record selection is exacerbated by the need to notify multiple participants when holdings are attached to the wrong record.

As an early union list project, PaULS also had to cope with technical problems caused by records tapeloaded into the Online Union Catalog. In an attempt to enrich the database, OCLC batchloaded bibliographic data in machine-readable form obtained from a variety of sources. While the goal of increasing the number of bibliographic records for serials was realized, new problems were created. For example, in some cases it was often hard to determine whether a record represented latest or successive entry cataloging. In other instances, as the bibliographic description was scant, difficulty arose in establishing the correct record in cases of non-unique titles. Some records were not clearly designated as representing microform, when in fact they were descriptions of microfilm. This was true, for example, in the case of all titles in the *American Periodical Series*. While patterns eventually emerged allowing correction or invalidation of erroneous records, many holdings statements were reported incorrectly before adequate quality control measures were in place.

Holdings data for PaULS participants were entered into OCLC's Serials Control Subsystem before development of fields designed specifically for summary holdings data. This step was taken after an agreement was reached between OCLC and PaULS staff providing for machine manipulation of the data as software to complete the union list capability was developed. The decision to proceed under these circumstances resulted in a non-standard reporting system that created problems peculiar to PaULS.[6,7] A fully functional union list capability on OCLC was not available until 1980. Application of a non-standard format for PaULS data entry, coupled with unanticipated delays in OCLC's conversion of that data to the standard format significantly hampered efforts to decentralize maintenance.

Consistent reporting of holdings data is an important technical issue for every union list group. While ambiguity has long existed regarding conventions for reporting serial holdings, two issues merit comment: (1) reporting holdings on microformat; and (2) the level of detail permissible in a holdings statement. With the continued development of OCLC's union listing capability, the publication of the *American National Standard for Serial Holdings State-*

ments (ANSI Z39.44-1986), and the official withdrawal of the *American National Standard for Serial Holdings Statements at the Summary Level* (ANSI Z39.42-1980), standards have evolved to the point where most reporting needs can be accommodated. Perhaps just as importantly, standards have continued to gain a wider acceptance in libraries participating in union list groups.

When the PaULS project was initiated, OCLC recommended that holdings statements for serials published in various formats be attached to the bibliographic description representing the appropriate format. Therefore, if an institution held a serial title in printed form, microfilm, and microfiche, respective holdings were attached to three different bibliographic records. In the case of PaULS, this convention increased substantially the need for entry of original records representing microformats. Strict application of the rule for reporting multiple formats fragmented holdings data and required multiple look-ups to determine complete institutional holdings. PaULS participants attended to this problem by adding a note to each local data record indicating whether additional holdings were available in other formats.

Holdings scatter is a condition inherent in union lists representing more than one library. Inconsistent reporting practices are often not normalized to achieve collocation of holdings data. While this problem is certainly not new or unique to PaULS, conversion of data to OCLC's union list component underscored the inefficiencies, both in time and cost, of multiple look-ups.

The need to create many new bibliographic records presented yet another difficulty for the PaULS project. With the implementation of AACR2 by LC in 1981 and a strict PaULS policy calling for adherence to national standards, new records created for microformats were prepared according to AACR2 conventions. However, many of the bibliographic records for the same serial title in printed form were prepared using earlier cataloging codes. Presence of bibliographic records for the same title in different physical manifestations created under a variety of cataloging rules sometimes resulted in holdings data attached to records with markedly different main entries. This discrepancy can usually be dismissed in an online file. The impact of offline products, however, is devastating.

An exception policy was established by OCLC in 1981 that permitted holdings in microformat to be attached to the bibliographic description representing the printed form.[8] Until 1983, few union list groups exercised this option. Increasingly, however, union list groups choose the option of attaching all holdings to a single bibliographic record. In fact, most active PaULS participants now opt for a consolidated holdings statement attached to the bibliographic record representing hard copy. While adopting this practice has generated efficiencies in both time and cost, it has also created incompatibilities in the PaULS database.

From a resource sharing perspective, consistent interpretation and application of standards for reporting holdings data are critical. Two provisions of ANSI Standard Z39.42-1980, one controlling the reporting of gaps and the other limiting the level of specificity permitted in holdings statements, have created inconsistencies in maintenance performed in a decentralized mode. This standard requires positive recording and display of holdings data (Standard Z39.42-1980 Section 1.2.2.). That is, institutions should report what is actually owned, not what is lacked. More specifically, according to the now obsolete Z39.42-1980, an institution was instructed to report ownership of a volume only if it held 50% or more of the published issues. Inconsistent application of this provision has been noted by interlibrary loan staff encountering unfilled requests (volume not held) for holdings positively reported in the union list. While no data exist to demonstrate definitively that requests go unfilled as a result of parochial application of the 50% rule, informal surveys suggest that few union list participants have been aware of this reporting convention.

ANSI Standard Z39.44-1986 prescribes the reporting of gaps in a summary holdings statement in a manner different from that prescribed by Z39.42-1980. According to the new standard (Z39.44-1986), reporting of gaps shall be based on whether or not any portion of a bibliographic unit is held by the reporting library (Standard Z39.44-1986 Section 7.2.4). While few libraries have implemented the provisions of ANSI Standard Z39.44-1986, an effort must be made to reconcile old reporting patterns with new if an additional inconsistency in PaULS reporting is to be avoided.

Closely connected to the issue of what to report is the level of specificity of holdings reported. ANSI Standard Z39.42-1980 was designed as a summary holdings standard. Therefore, institutions were instructed in most cases to report only the highest level of enumeration and chronology. A number of PaULS participants questioned the usefulness of holdings reported at the summary level. In fact, some institutions opted to report routinely two levels of enumeration. Other institutions added a note to each holdings statement detailing which volumes were incomplete. ANSI Standard Z39.44-1986 has resolved this problem by providing options and guidelines for reporting detailed holdings statements.

If applied consistently, limited divergence from standards does not constitute a problem. For example, the addition of notes specifying incomplete volumes probably does not have a profound effect on either system manipulation or interpretation of holdings data. However, in a decentralized environment it is difficult to ensure that all participants apply exceptions routinely and uniformly. The recent issue of ANSI Standard Z39.44-1986 represents an opportunity to reimpose uniformity on union list holdings. It is the responsibility of each union list group to retrofit whenever practical to provide consistent and reliable holdings data.

Financial Issues

A cornerstone for any successful union list project is adequate funding. Many large union lists are initiated with grant money, typically administered through state agencies. As a project moves into a decentralized mode, however, issues of funding must be examined to identify a practical and acceptable balance between state and local funds. In the case of PaULS, some local institutions have assumed a portion of the maintenance costs, when the benefits of maintaining union list data are clearly recognizable. This value judgment is based ordinarily on the availability of useful offline products. To a large extent, however, the state has continued to support PaULS maintenance.

Instructional and Motivational Issues

From a network perspective, training is fundamental to the success of any union list project. The importance of training and documentation that are readily available, relevant, and of high quality cannot be overestimated. Inadequate training invariably produces less than satisfactory results. A comprehensive training effort and a procedures manual were integral to the overall plan for PaULS. However, neither the training nor documentation was sufficient to encourage active participation.

To be effective, training must be relevant, focus on tasks as specific to the actual situation as possible, and include practice in an online mode. Training must also represent an opportunity to gain knowledge and skills that generate tangible results and identifiable rewards for both the trainee and the institution. Given the magnitude and geographical spread of PaULS participants, it was impractical for the regional networks in Pennsylvania to provide individual training for PaULS participants. While group training sessions were held throughout the PALINET service area over a period of three years, the sessions were not held frequently enough, could not include hands-on activity, and often required significant travel to attend. Moreover, because of the size of training groups, attention to individual problems was limited.

Training efforts were complicated by the fact that staff responsible for maintaining serial holdings data were often unfamiliar with the structure of the OCLC database, searching techniques, and the MARC-S format. In addition to instruction covering the ANSI Standard and OCLC's union list component, many participants also required basic system training. Time restrictions and fiscal constraints resulted in training inadequate to prepare staff to undertake maintenance work. Finally, unavailability of regular access to the OCLC System by serials personnel often prevented reinforcement of the skills learned and impeded PaULS maintenance.

The training issues outlined above appear to be typical of large union list groups attempting decentralized maintenance. While problems relating to local terminal accessibility cannot be solved at the network level, issues concerning frequency and design of training opportunities can be addressed in the planning stages of a union list project. Specifically, sufficient funds must be earmarked for regularly sponsored training opportunities. Training should be held at sites where terminal time can be made available for online activity. Attendees should be encouraged to read available documentation, complete pre-workshop exercises, and arrive at the training session with a list of titles that require online updating. In addition, the network must ensure that every participating institution receives an authorization number valid for union list maintenance activity. Finally, documentation which is clear, concise, and easy to use must be available to participating libraries.

Motivational Issues

Motivation is important to the success of any resource sharing initiative. Benefits must be identifiable and measurable. In the early stages of PaULS, generation of an offline product containing relatively current holdings data for titles frequently requested via interlibrary loan was among the desirable results of the project. However, in the longer term, lack of a convenient interface between interlibrary loan and union list data as well as insufficient training in accessing and interpreting online union list data discouraged many interlibrary loan staff from utilizing PaULS as a locator tool. The case can be made that lack of use by ILL staff served as a disincentive for serials personnel to maintain the data.

Fortunately, new incentives to access union list data online have been introduced over the past several years. An interface now exists permitting direct access to union list data when logged on to OCLC's Interlibrary Loan subsystem. This link produces a union group display in response to a single command issued from the ILL Subsystem. In addition, union list holdings, including volume specific institutional holdings, can be viewed at a lower cost than can institutional level, non-volume specific display.

III. THE LESSONS AND THE FUTURE

Putting the Experience to Work

PALINET's association with the PaULS project yielded valuable lessons and insights into the process of developing and promoting a statewide union list. The experience was put to work recently in the planning and creation of a statewide union list in New Jersey.

The environment and circumstances surrounding the conversion of the New Jersey Union List of Serials (NJULS) to OCLC differed markedly from those of the PaULS project. A statewide union list for New Jersey libraries had existed for a number of years before the conversion effort was undertaken. Therefore, libraries were accustomed to reporting to a central list. Moreover, by 1984 when the NJULS project was initiated, the Online Union Catalog contained over a half million serial records, many upgraded and authenticated by CONSER libraries.

However, lessons gleaned from the PaULS project as well as the project to create the New York Consolidated Union List of Serials (NYCON) via OCLC were valuable in the planning and implementation of the NJULS project. Following is a brief summary of key points.

An advisory committee was appointed early in the NJULS planning stages, and this was involved actively in developing priorities, recommendations, and policies for the project. Recognizing that momentum is an important variable in a successful union list project, one of the priorities of the NJULs project was rapid data conversion. Hence, the conversion of over 90,000 holdings statements representing approximately 27,500 titles held in 65 libraries was completed in nine months.

Issues related to offline product generation, funding, and training were addressed in the planning cycle. As a result, substantial LSCA funds have been allocated for continued development of the NJULS, and an offline product containing all holdings converted during the project's first phase was generated and distributed widely within one year of project initiation. An ongoing series of training sessions has also been established. Held twice each month and alternating between locations in the northern and southern regions of the state, these sessions are designed to provide hands-on experience in maintenance activity.

The conversion phase of the NJULS was managed capably and completed quickly and successfully. Libraries in the state are enthusiastic about the project and recognize the benefits of a comprehensive, up-to-date union list. At this point, decentralization of maintenance is in its early stages. It will be interesting, when the time comes, to compare the progress of this transition with the experience of PaULS.

Prognosis on the Future of PaULS

What then is the prognosis for PaULS in the years ahead? During the past two years, union list activity in Pennsylvania has increased steadily. PaULS is experiencing a renaissance within the framework of regional resource sharing programs. This is a particularly striking development. One of the major issues identified by the PaULS advisory committee for resolution during the transition stage from centralized input to decentralized maintenance of PaULS was the ". . . relationship of small union list groups to PaULS as a whole."[8]

A continued commitment to the PaULS database by the State Library of Pennsylvania has provided funds for a number of local union list projects. Between October 1985 and June 1987, over 53,000 new holdings statements have been added to the PaULS database, and more than 14,500 holdings statements have been updated as a result of grassroots initiatives. As of May 1987, the PaULS database contained 93,590 unique titles and 312,322 holding locations.

Regional union list groups in Pennsylvania currently participating in the development of online union lists of serials via OCLC include the *ACLCP Union List of Serials* group, a cooperative of 16 academic libraries in central Pennsylvania and the State Library; the *LVAIC Union List of Serials* group, a consortium of five academic libraries in Pennsylvania's Lehigh Valley; the *NEPBC/HILNNEP Union List of Serials* group, a multi-type cooperative comprising academic, public, and special libraries in the Scranton-Wilkes Barre area; and TCLC, a cooperative of 27 libraries in the greater Philadelphia area. In addition, a special grant to the Philadelphia College of Pharmacy and Science has resulted in the addition to PaULS of holdings for many highly specialized and sometimes obscure pharmacological titles. Collectively, the work of these groups has enriched the PaULS database substantially.

Of particular note is the fact that several of the regional union list groups have opted to be profiled as individual subsets while retaining their membership in PaULS. Searching for holdings at the regional level first often yields a location and results in more efficient document delivery. Utilizing the regional list as the primary source also promotes and reinforces previously developed patterns of library cooperation. When a request cannot be filled locally, group members search the larger PaULS file.

Finally, the Pennsylvania Newspaper Project, underway since 1985, has added a new dimension to the statewide union list. To date, over 16,500 locations for newspaper titles, many reported for the first time, have been added to the online union list. Many of the repositories inventoried as part of the project are also participants in the PaULS project.

Despite a period of reduced activity, PaULS is awakening with renewed vigor. As a product of pre-existing resource sharing arrangements, as well as of Pennsylvania's commitment to statewide and national cooperative projects, the revitalized PaULS database is becoming a primary and comprehensive locator tool for libraries throughout the Commonwealth.

NOTES

1. Ruth C. Carter, "Steps Toward an On-Line Union List," *Journal of Library Automation* 11(1):32-33 (March 1978).
2. Ruth C. Carter and Scott Bruntjen, "The Pennsylvania Union List of Serials: Initial Development," *The Serials Librarian* 5(3): 58-59 (Spring 1981).
3. Ruth C. Carter and Scott Bruntjen, "The Pennsylvania Union List of Serials: From Development to Maintenance," *The Serials Librarian* 8(4): 58-59 (Summer 1984).
4. Carter and Bruntjen, "The Pennsylvania Union List of Serials: Initial Development," 59-61.
5. While many PaULS member institutions did not undertake regular maintenance of union list data, there were several significant exceptions, among which were the University of Pittsburgh, Carnegie-Mellon University, and West Virginia University.
6. Carter, "Steps Toward," 39.
7. Carter and Bruntjen, "The Pennsylvania Union List of Serials: From Development to Maintenance," 57-59.
8. OCLC. *Serials Control User Manual* (1983), A:29-30.

Annotated Bibliography of Online Union Lists of Serials, 1979-1987

James D. Hooks, MLS, PhD

Items in the bibliography were selected based on consideration of the following criteria:

1. Regional and system online union lists of serials.
2. North American geographic area.
3. Publication data between 1979 and 1987.

The scope is broad-based and selections range from news articles to research projects.

Amelung, Richard, joint author.
    See Marilyn K. Nicely
        "MAUL: An OCLC Union List of Legal Periodicals."

Angus, Henrietta. "Pennsylvania Union List of Serials: Selection of Bibliographic Records." *Pittsburgh Regional Library Center Technical Bulletin*. (January 1986): 47-48.
Bibliographic record selection is essential for union list integrity. General rules for record selection are presented, and a sample entry is included.

Battistella, Maureen S. and Patricia M. Rodgers. "Role of a Health Library Association in the Development and Coordination of a Statewide Union List of Health Science Serials." *The Serials Librarian*. 11, no. 2 (October 1986): 75-81.
This article describes the formation of the Alabama Biomedical Union List of Serials under the egis of the Alabama Health Libraries

Association (AlHeLA). Initial data entry costs were underwritten by the Southeastern/Atlantic Region Medical Library Services (RMLS2). A survey was conducted to determine the need for a union list. Although the National Library of Medicine (NLM) based SERial HOLDings (SERHOLD) provided an initial union base, expansion would be necessary for resource sharing and interlibrary loan purposes. The authors discuss union list governance, communications, quality control, continuing education, and recruitment. In conclusion, it is noted that union list development has been adversely affected by the OCLC-based union list component. "A proposed OCLC-SERHOLD link will facilitate data exchange between the two union lists . . ." A sample entry and references are included.

Bell, Christine L. "A SERLINE-based Union List of Serials for Basic Health Sciences Libraries: A Detailed Protocol." *Medical Library Association. Bulletin of the Medical Library Association.* 70, no. 4 (October 1982): 380-388.
This union list project was initiated in 1981 by the Massachusetts Health Sciences Library network (MaHSLiN). The basis for the union list would stem from the six health-related consortia representing 116 libraries statewide. The Consortium for Information Resources (CIR) would bear the union list responsibility. Four factors were considered in union list creation: type of automation, form of bibliographic entry, form of the holdings statement, and procedures for updating. Since full SERLINE records would not be necessary, the union list would be based on selected elements from the SERLINE bibliographic entry. The author also discusses budget, financing, and protocols. Charts, tables, and sample entries are provided, and bibliographic references are included.

Bell, Christine L. "A SERLINE-based Union List of Serials for Basic Health Sciences Libraries: An Update Experience." *Medical Library Association. Bulletin of the Medical Library Association.* 72, no. 1 (January 1984): 26-28.
The author discusses changes in the second edition of the Union List of Serials (ULS-II) in the Massachusetts Health Sciences Library Network (MaHSLiN). The major areas of focus are proce-

dural changes, processing changes, printing charges, and budget and finance. The SERLINE-based ULS-II "has proved to be an efficient, cost-effective, and desirable format for the consolidation of biomedical journal holdings at the basic level of health sciences libraries." Tables and bibliographic references are included.

Blixrud, Julia, joint author.
    See Marjorie E. Bloss
        "Guidelines for Union Lists of Serials."

Bloss, Marjorie E. "And in Hindsight . . . The Past Ten Years of Union Listing." *The Serials Librarian*. 10 (Fall 1985/Winter 1985-86): 141-148.

Computer technology has made online serials databases feasible. This has been made evident through the CONSER project, OCLC, Faxon LINX, and other bibliographic networks. In addition, both ALA and IFLA have given attention to the establishment of union list guidelines. Future developments are mentioned.

Bloss, Marjorie. "The Dregs in the Union List Bottle: Titles Not in the Database." *Serials Review*. 10, no. 2 (Summer 1984): 49-53.

A general background for the Rochester 3Rs Union List of Serials is provided as well as a brief description of its centralized union list operation. Bibliographic record selection is discussed and extensive detail is given concerning the handling and cataloging of surrogate titles not in the OCLC database.

Bloss, Marjorie E., and others. *Guidelines for Union Lists of Serials*. Serials Section, Resources and Technical Services Division, [Chicago]: American Library Association, 1982, 52pp. (OCLC no. 9230327)

The purpose of this document is to provide a descriptive approach to the creation, production, and maintenance of union lists of serials. It was prepared to meet a growing need for general information about union lists. "The GUIDELINES are not . . . standards for creating, producing, or maintaining union lists." The project methodology is outlined, and a conclusion, glossary, bibliography, and index are included.

Bloss, Marjorie E. "The Impact of AACR2 on Union Lists of Serials." *Cataloging & Classification Quarterly*. 3, nos. 2/3 (Winter 1982/Spring 1983): 97-109.

Union lists of serials are for the most part location devices, not cataloging tools. As such full bibliographic records are not generally needed and may even be a hindrance to the union list purpose. While online data will mostly conform to CONSER standards, offline products will be a different matter. AACR2 rules that will have the greatest impact on union lists are descriptive cataloging, choice of entry for microreproductions, successive entry, initialisms, and uniform titles. Bibliographic references are provided.

Bloss, Marjorie E. "In Order to Form a More Perfect Union . . . List of Serials." In *The Management of Serials Automation: Current Technology & Strategies for Future Planning*. Edited with an introduction by Peter Gellatly. New York: The Haworth Press, 1982, 191-197.

This paper describes the formation of the ALA Ad Hoc Committee on Union List of Serials. Five major concerns are presented: (1) basic principles of union lists, (2) determining union list responsibility, (3) union list content, (4) data collection and distribution, and (5) evaluation and ongoing maintenance. Future concerns are noted.

Bloss, Marjorie E. "In Order to Form a More Perfect Union . . . List of Serials: A Report of the Workshop." *Serials Review*. 8, no. 1 (Spring 1982): 67-68.

Events of the union list workshop held at the ALA conference in San Francisco are noted. "The program was developed because union lists of serials suddenly seem to be cropping up . . . [and] focused on the practical aspects of creating, compiling and producing a union list of serials." Speakers were Jean Whiffen, Dorothy Glasby, Virginia Boucher, Elaine Woods, Julia Blixrud, Mary Moules, Dianne Ellsworth, Dea Szatkowski, and Ruth Carter.

Bloss, Marjorie E. "Quality Control: Centralized and Decentralized Union Lists." *Serials Review*. 8, no. 3 (Fall 1982): 89-95.

This is one of three papers presented at a special SUNY/OCLC session in April 1982. The author advocates centralized union list maintenance as the preferred way to ensure quality control. Numerous observations from the Rochester 3R's Project are provided, and union list statistics are included. Quality control of staff, microforms, and holdings statements are also discussed. Bibliographic notes are provided.

Bloss, Marjorie E. "The Serials Pastiche: Union Lists of Serials." *Drexel Library Quarterly*. 21 (Winter 1985): 100-111.
The concept of union lists is presented in an historical context, and the rationale for their development is evidenced in the way they impinge on all areas of library service. Administrative and financial concerns are noted, and the centralization versus decentralization debate is given attention. Advantages and disadvantages of offline products are discussed briefly. Ongoing maintenance is stressed as a much needed activity for union list stability.

Bloss, Marjorie E. "Uniformity in Union Lists of Serials: Measuring Up to Standards." In *Library Serials Standards: Development, Implementation, Impact: Proceedings of the Third Annual Serials Conference*. Edited by Nancy Jean Melin. Westport, CT: Meckler, 1984, 61-70.
Online bibliographic access to standard records permits union list editors to elect desired elements for union list display. The author proposes eight basic union list components: main entry, title, uniform title, edition, numeric/chronological designations, place of publication/distribution, publisher/distributor, and notes. Details are given concerning the development of ANSI standards. Additional information regarding the efforts of ISO (International Standards Organization) and IFLA to formulate international standards is provided.

Bloss, Marjorie E. "Union Lists of Serials' Futures: Buy? Sell? or Keep What You've Got?" *Technical Services Quarterly*. 1, nos. 1/2 (Fall/Winter 1983): 159-170.
A union list can exist only by cooperation of its participants. This article raises issues concerning the survival of union lists: namely, will there be a need for these in the year 2000? And, if so, how will they compare with the union lists of today? Centralization versus decentralization as a method of union list maintenance is examined.

Also CONSER, AACR2, and MARC-S guidelines are considered as standardized components of union listing projects. The impact of the electronic journal is noted. Bibliographic references are included.

Bowen, Johanna E. "The Management of Quality Control in a Decentralized Union Listing Project." *Serials Review*. 8, no. 3 (Fall 1982): 87-88.

This is one of three papers presented at a special SUNY/OCLC session in April 1982. The author describes various steps in the South Central Research Library Council (SCRLC) union list project which involved 53 libraries. The project was supported with LSCA funds through the New York State Library. The SCRLC is viewed as a part of the larger proposed New York Serials (NYSER) database. Steps taken to implement the SCRLC union list project are outlined, and quality control issues are addressed.

Bowen, Johanna E. "Report of The Serials Online Union List Users Group (SOUL)." *Serials Review*. 12, no. 4 (Winter 1986): 87.

The activities of the June 28, 1986 meeting of SOUL are reported. The use of US-MARC holdings format was discussed, and OCLC's future plans for online serials participants were heard: MARC holdings format, four-letter institution codes, user friendly menus, and union list capabilities.

Boyce, Bert R., joint author.
    See Judith I. Boyce
        "A Serials Holding List . . ."

Boyce, Judith I. and Bert R. Boyce. "A Serial Holding List Using UNIX Refer." *Special Libraries*. 78, no. 1 (Winter 1987): 37-40.

This article describes the successful utilization of UNIX-based Refer software to produce camera-ready union list copy. The need for a new printed union list arose as a result of holdings changes and closing in some of LaGIN (Louisiana Government Information Network) libraries. The Louisiana State Library with assistance from the Louisiana State University School of Library and Information Science supported the project. The authors note that while current union list access is through the printed list, online access may be more desirable in the future. Bibliographic references are included.

Bruntjen, Scott. "Purchase a Massive Union List." *Pittsburgh Regional Library Center Newsletter.* no. 97 (December 1984): [1-3].
A summary of the development and production of the Pennsylvania Union List of Serials is presented. Descriptive statistics regarding PaULS are provided. Questions and answers about PaULS and sample entries are included.

Bruntjen, Scott and Ruth C. Carter. "Pennsylvania Union List of Serials: A Description." *The Serials Librarian.* 4, no. 2 (Winter 1979): 257-258.
The authors describe plans for an online union list of serials in Pennsylvania (PaULS) to be supported by LSCA Title-III funds. The PaULS project was an outgrowth of a statewide study, *Bibliographic Access in Pennsylvania*. The initial project focused around a core list of approximately 2,000 titles. PRLC (Pittsburgh Regional Library Center) would serve as the project agent, and OCLC was chosen as the bibliographic utility. Centralized and decentralized maintenance are noted.

Bruntjen, Scott and Ruth Carter. "Serials Cancellations: Taking Advantage of Online Union Lists." *Wilson Library Bulletin.* 59 (October 1984): 103-105.
Both the need for serial cancellations and the desirability of an effective method to make such cancellations are addressed. The use of online union lists for serials management is illustrated by the results of the Pittsburgh Regional Library Center serials cancellation project. This project, supported by a grant from the Council on Library Resources, demonstrated that resource sharing maintenance can be accomplished via an online database.

Bruntjen, Scott
   See Pennsylvania Union List of Serials: Core Titles.

Bruntjen, Scott, joint author.
   See Ruth C. Carter
      "Serials Cancellation Project. Final Report."

Burkholder, Sue A. "Missouri Union List Review." *Show-Me Libraries*. 33, no. 6 (March 1982): 15-17.

This article describes the availability and utility of printed editions of the Missouri Union List of Serial Publications (MULSP). MULSP contains 39,710 titles with 113,992 holdings statements from 106 participating libraries. The author also discusses other applications of the union list database and notes the potential for machine readable magnetic tapes. Online access to MULSP is available from 17 terminals across the state and is especially useful as a location tool for interlibrary loan requests. Union list development will continue to play a central role in resource sharing among Missouri libraries.

Carter, Ruth C. "Cataloging Decisions on Pre-AACR2 Serial Records from a Union List Viewpoint." *Serials Review*. 7, no. 2 (April/June 1981): 77-78.

This article emphasizes adherence to national standards as a basic commitment to union list projects. The author uses experiences from the University of Pittsburgh catalog, the Pittsburgh Regional Library Center union list, and the Pennsylvania Union List of Serials. The treatment of pre-AACR2 records and latest versus successive entries are discussed.

Carter, Ruth C. "Pennsylvania Union List of Serials." *OCLC Newsletter*. no. 145 (February 1983): 9.

This article reports on the progress of the Pennsylvania Union List of Serials following the conversion of the PaULS database to the OCLC required union list format. Union listing commitment is to be shared by the University of Pittsburgh, Pittsburgh Regional Library Center, Pennsylvania Library Network, and State Library of Pennsylvania.

Carter, Ruth C. and Scott Bruntjen. *Serials Cancellation Project. Final Report*. Pittsburgh Regional Library Center, 1983. (ERIC Document no. 238-452)

This final report presents eighteen conclusions and six recommendations for future action that proceeded from a serials cancellation pilot project conducted by PRLC from August 1981 to December 1983. Sample forms, correspondence, workshop materials, acquisition questionnaire, PaULS printouts, and a list of project participants are included.

Carter, Ruth C.
See Pennsylvania Union List of Serials: Core Titles.

Carter, Ruth C., joint author.
See Scott Bruntjen
"Pennsylvania Union List of Serials: A Description."

Carter, Ruth C., joint author.
See Scott Bruntjen
"Serials Cancellations: Taking Advantage of Online Union Lists."

Charbonneau, Gary and others. *Examples of Holdings Reports and Decisions Using the American National Standard for Serial Holdings Statements at the Summary Level.* Bloomington: Indiana University, 1983. (ERIC Document no. 232-701)
The focus of this paper is the application of ANSI standards to the development, funded by a USOE Higher Education Act Title II-C grant, of an online union list of serials for the Indiana University Libraries. The authors report that while the work to convert holding records to ANSI format is not complicated, it "demands a high degree of understanding, consistency, and attention to detail." Examples are provided.

Chatterton, Leigh A. "The Boston College Libraries: A Case Study in Serials Automation." *Serials Review*. 10, no. 2 (Summer 1984): 65-71.
This article stems from a serials automation position paper developed for the Boston College Libraries (BCL) in February 1981. The findings of this study ultimately led to the purchase of a turnkey system to meet BCL's needs. BCL, which is partially decentralized, is made up of a number of libraries and divisions. The various steps taken to select a system are outlined: study and evaluation and systems requirements. Once a decision had been made to purchase the Faxon Linx System, other steps were necessary: proposal for purchase, funding, scheduling, and implementation. The author

concludes by discussing advantages and disadvantages of the system, public service benefits, and the current status of automation at BCL.

Cipolla, Wilma Reid, joint author.
>   See Marjorie E. Bloss
>   "Guidelines for Union Lists of Serials."

"Computerized Union Listing in New York State." *Wilson Library Bulletin*. 56, no. 9 (May 1982): 655.
This brief article announces that an agreement has been reached on the development of a New York State union list representing 124 institutions. Support for the union list project is from the New York State Library, OCLC, and SUNY/OCLC.

Conochie, Jean A. "Has Serials Union Listing Come of Age?: A Review of Four Recent Works on Union Listing." *The Serials Librarian*. 9, no. 4 (Summer 1985): 67-72.
Four sets of serials union listing guidelines are examined:
1. UNION LISTS OF SERIALS: GUIDELINES, MHSLN, 1981.
2. GUIDELINES FOR UNION LISTS OF SERIALS, ALA, 1982.
3. UNION CATALOGUES OF SERIALS: GUIDELINES FOR CREATION AND MAINTENANCE, WITH RECOMMENDED STANDARDS FOR BIBLIOGRAPHIC AND HOLDING CONTROL, Jean Whiffin, 1983.
4. GUIDELINES FOR THE COMPILATION OF UNION CATALOGUES OF SERIALS, IFLA, 1982.

The author compares these guidelines with specific reference to proper planning, bibliographic scope, and authority control. Bibliographic references are provided.

De Buse, Ray. "Washington Library Network." In *Union Lists: Issues and Answers*. Edited by Dianne Ellsworth. Ann Arbor, MI: The Pierian Press, 1982, 50-52.
The Washington Library Network (WLN) began in 1977 with 56 libraries in Alaska, Idaho, Oregon, Washington, and Montana. It has expanded to 76 libraries or library systems, and its database exceeds 150,000 records in size. WLN online serials cataloging is

based on MARC-S entries and follows CONSER guidelines. Off-line COM and computer line printed lists can be generated.

Downing, Jeff. "Texas Union List of Serials Is Statewide." *OCLC Newsletter*. no. 157 (April 1985): 11.
The article provides a brief outline of the steps taken in developing a statewide union list using OCLC's Union List Component. Major funding was from an LSCA-III grant with the Texas State Library as the union list agent.

Dukes, Earnstein and Jane Qualls. "A Tennessee Union List of Serials—Is It Time?" *Tennessee Librarian*. 36, no. 3 (Summer 1984): 68-75.
The Tennessee union list project was based upon a questionnaire survey that was conducted statewide to determine the relevant need. Data collection and statistical methods are described. The questionnaire included sections on interlibrary loan activity, location verification sources, bibliographic verification sources, and participation by the respondents in union lists. Summary conclusions "suggest that a Tennessee union list of serials is needed and would be valuable to libraries." Tables are provided.

Dwyer, James R. "Evolving Serials, Evolving Access: Bibliographic Control of Serial Literature." *Serials Review*. 12, nos. 2-3 (Summer/Fall 1986): 59-64.
Online union listing activity and other technological advances will play a central role in serial developments of the 21st century, as will the arrival of the "online journal." While the creation of online union lists currently supports interlibrary loan, retrospective conversion, and cataloging, implications for future linking and integration are noted as a way to provide "direct end-user access." Bibliographic notes are included.

Ellsworth, Dianne. "California Library Authority for Systems and Services." In *Union Lists: Issues and Answers*. Edited by Dianne Ellsworth. Ann Arbor, MI: The Pierian Press, 1982, 17-22.
The author briefly presents the history of the California Union List of Periodicals (CULP) and explains union list maintenance. Online access is identified as a major concern. CULP is in its seventh edi-

tion and is supported by 620 libraries. It contains more than 72,000 titles.

Ellsworth, Dianne. "California Union List of Periodicals: A Report." *The Serials Librarian*. 4, no. 4 (Summer 1980): 484-486.

This article describes the event of a serials union list workshop sponsored by the technical services chapter of CLA. Various speakers provided information about the ANSI holdings format, the creation of a merged serials list for Standard, UCLA, and the University of California, Berkeley, the University of California Union List of Serials (UCLUS), and problems of standardization in California. Other discussion centered round choice and form of union list entry, bibliographic and holdings standards, multiple reporting and the role of public and special libraries, and CONSER developments.

Ellsworth, Dianne J. "Serials Union Lists." *Serials Review*. 5, no. 3 (July/September 1979): 99-101.

The focus of this article is the origin and development of the CONSER (Conversion of Serials) project and its impact on the creation of online union lists. An Ad Hoc Committee known as the "Toronto Group" provided the impetus and obtained funding from the Council on Library Resources. The Minnesota Union List of Serials would be used to establish the database, and OCLC would be chosen as the computer facility. Benefits to CONSER participants are noted, and a bibliography is included.

Ellsworth, Dianne J. "Serials Union Lists and Automation." *Serials Review*. 6, no. 1 (January/March 1980): 69-70.

This article describes a joint union list project of the three strongest research libraries in California: the University of California at Berkeley, Stanford University, and the University of California at Los Angeles. The project was funded by a three-year HEA Title-IIC grant. Its purpose was to make the collections of these libraries more widely accessible. Serials records were upgraded to MARC-S standards and either loaded or planned to be loaded into the RLIN database. With only one year of the project completed, over 120,000 serials records have undergone some phase of conversion.

Ellsworth, Dianne J. "Union List Access Using Online Reference Retrieval Software." *Serials Review*. 8, no. 4 (Winter 1982): 87-89.

This article describes the California Union List of Periodicals (CULP) project, which contains approximately 375,000 holdings records from more than 740 libraries in California. CULP was designed as a location tool and not intended for serials cataloging. Since CULP is available through BRS, titles may be searched with keywords and in multiple fields and thus is not limited to "exact form of entry" searching.

Ellsworth, Dianne J. and Edward Newman. "The California Union List of Periodicals." In *The Management of Serials Automation: Current Technology & Strategies for Future Planning*. Edited with an introduction by Peter Gellatly. New York: The Haworth Press, 1982, 199-217.

The history and background of the California Union List of Periodicals provides a focus for the development of an online database. The project was supported by LSCA Title-I funds and was administered by the California State Library. Holdings of 600 libraries are represented and the database contains 71,000 titles and approximately 340,000 holdings locations. Data collection, processing, production, and bibliographic concerns are examined. National standards and future developments are considered. The CULP Users Guide is included.

Ellsworth, Dianne, joint author.
   See Marjorie E. Bloss
      "Guidelines for Union Lists of Serials."

Fayad, Susan and Charlene D. Wecker. "The OCLC Union List Product: Michigan's Recommendation on Design Options." *Serials Review*. 10, no. 4 (Winter 1984): 69-87.

Various factors (record arrangement, bibliographical content, cross references, etc.) that have produced an impact on union list offline products in the Michigan Library Consortium are described. A wide range of union list options are discussed including subsets, configurations, and copy specific notes. A rationale for selecting certain options and sample formats are included.

Fayad, Susan, joint author.
> See Charlene D. Wecker
>> "The OCLC Union List Product: Evaluation & Critique of Michigan's Statewide Product."

Feiza, Carol, project clerk.
> See Serials of Illinois Libraries Online: Manual of Procedures.

Forsman, Rick B. "A Vendor-Supported Experiment in Union Listing." *The Serials Librarian.* 9 (Summer 1985): 73-82.
This article describes a local online union list experiment that was supported by a serials vendor. It involved five libraries in the Birmingham, Alabama, metropolitan area. During the test period problems and benefits were noted, and use information was collected and tabulated. Conclusions and future plans are discussed.

Gearty, Tom, joint author.
> See Barbara Settel
>> "An Online Union List of Serials . . ."

Green, Judy Gibson, joint author.
> See Marsha Kaiserman
>> "ULSSCL Is Joint Product of User and Publisher Effort."

Hartman, Anne-Marie. "The Implications of AACR2 On Serials management and Union Listing." In *Union Lists: Issues and Answers*. Edited by Dianne Ellsworth. Ann Arbor, MI: The Pierian Press, 1982, 71-76.
This presentation addresses the impact of AACR2 cataloging rules on union list projects, especially with regard to online entry. Although important questions are raised, the author notes that solutions are elusive.

Hartman, Anne-Marie. "Quality Control in a Decentralized Union List Using OCLC." *Serials Review.* 8, no.3 (Fall 1982): 88-89.
This is one of three papers presented at a special SUNY/OCLC session in April 1982. The City University of New York (CUNY)

union list project comprising 19 separate units is featured. The union list project agent is Queens College. Local training, ongoing quality control, and problems are examined.

Hawks, Mary. "Serials Union Listing in Arkansas—1983." *Arkansas Libraries*. 40, no. 3 (September 1983): 25-26.
The printed Arkansas Union List of Periodicals representing 29 participating libraries and managed by the Arkansas State University has provided the basis for OCLC online conversion. The conversion project was funded by an LSCA Title-III grant awarded by the Arkansas State Library. Future concerns of ongoing maintenance costs and establishment of a union list agent need to be addressed.

Hoffman, David R. "The Pennsylvania Newspaper Project: Initial Stages." *The Serials Librarian*. 10, no. 3 (Spring 1986): 69-76.
The author summarizes the background of the Pennsylvania Newspaper Project ad hoc committee and the "formally-constituted planning committee." Survey response from potential repositories is noted, and procedures for getting the project underway are discussed. Cataloging sites are described, and funding sources are mentioned. Maps showing the number of newspapers published by county are included.

Hooks, James D. "PaULS—A Location Enhancement for Interlibrary Loan." *Pittsburgh Regional Library Center Technical Bulletin*. (January 1986): 53.
The interlibrary loan office is a prime user of online union list information. The utilization of copy-specific holding information is critical in reducing turnaround time.

Hooks, James D. "Union Listing: A Reference Perspective." *OCLC Newsletter*. no. 156 (February 1985): 17.
This article is based on a paper presented at the 1984 Pittsburgh Regional Library Center Spring Conference. Dial access as a possible solution to union list maintenance is examined. Union list implications for reference/interlibrary loan service are noted.

"Indiana University Libraries Recently Announced That Agreement Had Been Reached With OCLC, Inc. of Columbus, OH on the Final Specifications for an On-Line Union List of Serials." *The Serials Librarian*. 4, no. 2 (Winter 1979): 250.

This article announces that Indiana University Libraries (Bloomington, Indiana) will begin its online union list project funded by a grant through the U.S. Office of Education Title II-C of the Higher Education Act. "The purpose of the grant is . . . to support the development of an on-line union list of serials capability using the OCLC, Inc. data base [and] to support the retrospective conversion of Indiana University's serial bibliographic records into MARC-S format." Project development began in November 1979, and the expected project test date was January 1980.

Kaiserman, Marsha and Judy Gibson Green. "ULSSCL Is Joint Product of User and Publisher Effort." *Canadian Library Journal*. 44, no. 1 (February 1987): 23-26.

The authors provide the background for the Union List of Scientific Serials in Canadian Libraries (ULSSCL) which is published by the Canadian Institute of Scientific and Technical Information (CISTI). The conversion to DOBIS project is described, including reporting methods and offline products. DOBIS is "an online shared cataloguing system jointly developed by the National Library of Canada and CISTI. The project resulted in adding 57,000 records to the DOBIS system. Examples and references are provided.

Kass, Tina. "Research Libraries Group." In *Union Lists: Issues and Answers*. Edited by Dianne Ellsworth. Ann Arbor, MI: The Pierian Press, 1982, 45-47.

This article describes the Research Libraries Group (RLG) RLIN system. This system contains 90,000 MARC records. In addition, about 70,000 records created by the Stanford University Libraries and 150,000 union list records from the University of California at Berkeley are available on RLIN.

Kozaczka, Stanley J. *The Polish Collection at the Alliance College Library in Cambridge Springs, PA: The Origins of the Collection in 1950, its Rapid Development in the 1970's and the Introduction of the Online Computer Library Center (OCLC) in 1982.* Cambridge Springs, PA: Alliance College, 1983, p. 14. (ERIC Document no. 235-823)

This essay outlines the participation of Alliance College in the Pennsylvania Union List of Serials project. Project participation was funded by a LSCA grant through the State Library of Pennsylvania.

Kraft, Nancy. "The Iowa Newspaper Project: A Field Report." *The Serials Librarian.* 12, nos. 1/2 (1987): 117-129.

The background of the Iowa Newspaper Project, which spans a 20-year period, is presented in this article. The project has largely been funded by the National Endowment for the Humanities and also, over the years has been supported by the Organization of American Historians, the State Historical Society of Iowa, the University of Iowa, and Iowa State University. The author discusses how the project was planned and implemented. Union list concerns are addressed, and the value of project publicity is noted. Reference notes are included.

Liu, Susana J. *Serials Automation for San Jose State University Library.* San Jose, CA: San Jose State University, 1980. [A Research Paper Presented to the Faculty of the School of Education, San Jose State University in Partial Fulfillment of the Requirements for the Degree Master of Arts.] (ERIC Document No. 194-097)

This paper examines the manual check-in procedures at San Jose State University and makes recommendations for designing a more efficient system. The author notes that while "serials can be controlled very efficiently in a manual operation," an automated online system would facilitate information retrieval, union list preparation, etc. The OCLC Serials Control Subsystem is discussed in considerable detail. A review of the literature, references, appendices, and examples are included.

Miller, Barbara. "Managing Input Routines." *Pittsburgh Regional Library Center Technical Bulletin.* (January 1986): 47.

Incorporating union list maintenance into the normal workflow process is suggested as a way to keep local data records current. Concern over the lack of local maintenance efforts is noted.

Montgomery, Teresa, joint author.
See Barbara Radke
"CALLS ISSN Project."

Moore, Brian P. "At ALA: Union Listing Users Group, Claiming Demonstrated." *OCLC Newsletter*. no. 148 (August 1983): 9.
The formal organization of the OCLC Union Listing Users Group is observed. The group heard reports on offline products and future documentation.

Moore, Brian P. "Union List Offline Products." *OCLC Newsletter*. no. 153 (June 1984): 9.
Offline union list products signal an important step in union list development. The first phase produced a paper format list. Microfiche, indexes, and tape products are expected to follow. A sample format is included.

Moore, Brian P. *Union List Update #6 – Revision*. Dublin, OH: OCLC, December 1, 1982, 8pp.
The report revises the Union List Update #6 following a review by the Union List Task Force on November 8, 1982. OCLC's interpretations of questions regarding various union list practices are set forth:

1. When to use second level enumeration or chronology?
2. When should enumeration and chronology be parallel?
3. How to report incomplete holdings?

The revisions noted in this report are to be incorporated into a new union list manual to be published by OCLC in summer, 1983. The use of captions and local notes are also examined. Numerous examples are provided.

Moore, Brian P. "Union Listing User Group to Form." *OCLC Newsletter*. no. 147 (June 1983): 8.
Significant growth in the OCLC Union Listing Component is observed since its availability in 1981. The formation of a union listing user group is noted.

Moules, Mary L. "Producing a Local Union List of Serials with Word Processing Equipment." *The Serials Librarian*. 7, no. 2 (Winter 1982): 27-34.

This article describes the development of the Illinois Valley Library System (IVLS) union list, a list that follows latest title entry rules. The author discusses the rationale for adopting latest versus successive title entry, title proper as the entry element, and holdings information. The IBM Office System-6, used to produce the union list, is examined, and final union list format is described. It is estimated that the IVLS Union List will contain 10,000 titles with a system maximum of 15,000 titles. In conclusion, it is noted that this approach to union listing best served the special needs of IVLS. Union list examples are provided.

"NEOMAL Builds Serials List of the Holdings of Nine Members." *Library Journal*. 107, no. 9 (May 1, 1982): 845.

This news release describes the union list activities of the Northeast Ohio Major Academic Libraries (NEOMAL) consortium. Participating members are identified, and union list objectives are noted.

Nelson, Norman. "Union List of Serials Project Under Way at OSU Library." *Oklahoma Librarian*. 30, no. 4 (October 1980): 9-10.

The article describes the 3rd edition of the Oklahoma Union List of Serials project. The project, funded by LSCA, will contain 40,000 records to be input into the OCLC database. Offline products will include print and microfiche editions. There will be 39 libraries participating in the project—12 special libraries, 22 academic libraries and 5 public libraries. Project responsibility rests with an administrative board of members from participating libraries. At the onset, inputting will be from a central office in the OSU Library. Later local inputting is planned.

New Jersey State Library. *A Report of the Computer Application Task Force*. Trenton: New Jersey State Library, 1980, p. 14. (ERIC Document no. 234-766)

The expansion of the NJULS (New Jersey Union List of Serials) is one of several matters dealt with in this report, which stresses the utilization of computer technology to support library development in New Jersey. The NJULS contains 59,000 titles from 131 libraries. The Task Force recommends online data entry and editing terminals to facilitate database expansion.

Newman, Edward, joint author.
   See Dianne J. Ellsworth
      "The California Union List of Periodicals."

Nicely, Marilyn K., Kaye Stoppel, and Richard Amelung. "MAUL: An OCLC Union List of Legal Periodicals." *Law Library Journal*. 76, no. 2 (Spring 1983): 394-401.
The Mid America Law School Library Consortium includes 18 law libraries in 7 midwestern states. In 1982 the consortium authorized the creation of an online union list using the OCLC union list component. AMIGOS was selected as the union list agent. The authors discuss union listing on OCLC, implementation, offline products, and union list evaluation. Future concerns are noted. The article is well illustrated. Appendices describe record selection and local data record creation.

"OCLC-Based Union List in N.Y. Is Step Towards OCLC/RLIN Link." *Library Journal*. 107, no. 10 (May 15, 1982): 925-926.
This is a brief announcement of the negotiated agreement of the State University of New York/OCLC network, the New York State Library, and OCLC to develop a statewide union list for resource sharing. The New York State Library will serve as the union list agent.

O'Malley, Terrence J. "Union Listing Via OCLC's Serials Control Subsystem." *Special Libraries*. 75, no. 75 (April 1984): 131-150.
The OCLC Serials Control Subsystem is examined in relationship to CONSER. CONSER purpose and objectives are noted. The author draws upon experiences from the Northeast Ohio Major Academic Libraries (NEOMAL) union list. Summary copy holdings (SCHD) and summary institution holdings (SIHD) fields are explained, and the importance of proper union list record selection is

emphasized. This article is well illustrated with examples and sample entries. Literature cited is included.

"Online Union Listing Users are Enthusiastic." *OCLC Bulletin.* (November 1981): 3+.
Based on an interview with Ron Gardner, OCLC Instructional Coordinator, the article emphasizes the benefits and advantages of an online union list, especially noting the ease of updating local data records. A directory of union list groups is included.

Osmus, Lori L. "Serials Cataloging from the Union List Standpoint." *The Serials Librarian.* 12, nos. 1/2 (1987): 101-116.
This article focuses on the union list as a finding tool. As such, "the impact of different cataloging rules on bibliographic description is not as serious as it is for choice and form of entry." However, guidelines for access points must be well defined and adhered to if an online union list database is to be developed consistently and in a manner that will benefit its users. The author also addresses other issues: successive versus latest entry, microforms, record selection, and advantages of online union listing. In conclusion, a number of unanswered union list questions are raised that will ultimately have to be dealt with. Discrepancies which occur in the union list usually have to be resolved by the union list editor. Bibliographic notes and references are provided.

Pearson, Karl M. *CULP (California Union List of Periodicals) 1980 User Survey Results.* San Jose, CA: California Library Authority for Systems and Services, 1981. (ERIC Document no. 200-224)
This study, supported in part by LSCA funds, summarizes survey questionnaire data of 391 out of 696 participating CULP libraries using the CULP microfiche union list of periodicals. The positive response to question 6 regarding a "searchable online file" supports future developments in that direction.

Pennsylvania Union List of Serials. [Dublin, Ohio]: OCLC 1984, 8619 pp. OCLC#12181486.
This is the first offline hard copy edition of the *Pennsylvania Union List of Serials*, which includes more than 80,000 titles reported by

287 participating libraries located in Pennsylvania, West Virginia, Western Maryland, Delaware, and New Jersey. This edition was preceded by a microfiche copy produced in 1982. The project was supported by the Pittsburgh Regional Library Center, PALINET, and the State Library of Pennsylvania.

Pennsylvania Union List of Serials: Core Titles. [Microfiche] Edited by Timothy Sperry; with an introduction by Ruth C. Carter and Scott Bruntjen. Pittsburgh, PA: Pittsburgh Regional Library Center, 1982. OCLC#8773851.

This is the first COM (Computer Output Microfiche) offline product of the *Pennsylvania Union List of Serials (PaULS)*. It contains 2,580 core titles held among more than 250 participating libraries in Pennsylvania, West Virginia, and Western Maryland, Delaware, and New Jersey. The core list contains a selected portion of more than 80,000 titles and 400,000 holdings which are online in the OCLC database. The project was made possible by the combined efforts of participating libraries, the Pittsburgh Regional Library Center, PALINET, and the State Library of Pennsylvania. A four-letter institutional holding code list is provided.

Preston, Jenny. "Missouri Union List of Serial Publications." *The Serials Librarian*. 5, no. 1 (Fall 1980): 65-77.

The Missouri Union List of Serial Publications began as the St. Louis Union List of Periodicals. In 1977 a second LSCA Title-III grant was awarded to create a statewide online union list. A brief history is provided. The union list project is administered by the Technical Services Division of the St. Louis Public Library and "emphasis is placed on structured network participation." Major concerns are examined: online participation, automation, staffing, bibliographic records, and editorial consistency. The author concludes by noting the possibility of future use of a full MARC entry, more varied offline products, and a statewide machine-readable database.

Qualls, Jane, joint author.
    See Earnstein Dukes
        "A Tennessee Union List of Serials—Is It Time?"

Radke, Barbara and Teresa Montgomery. "CALLS ISSN Project." *Serials Review*. 8, no. 2 (Summer 1982): 65-67.

The CALLS ISSN project began in 1980. It was funded by HEA Title II-C. The California Academic Libraries List of Serials (CALLS) wanted to determine the feasibility of using the ISSN to sort and merge serial records input from various locations and/or sources. The experiment sample failed to meet the conditions necessary for use of the ISSN in that manner. The authors note that the ISSN may prove to be useful as an "access point for on-line retrieval."

Rast, Elaine K. "Serials in Illinois Libraries On-line (SILO)." *Illinois Libraries*. 65, no. 5 (May 1983) 348-350. [Volume on inside page differs from cover—v.64, no.5.]

The author presents a brief outline of resource sharing in Illinois from 1965 to date. As the union list project got underway, a union list subcommittee of the Illinois State Library was established, and OCLC was chosen as the union list vendor. The project, funded by an LSCA grant through the Illinois State Library Advisory Committee, included 61 participating libraries. Union list headquarters was established at Northern Illinois University. The author discusses the union list requirements considered for vendor selection, and the benefits of the union list project are noted. Footnotes are provided.

Rast, Elaine and John Tieberg-Bailie. "SILO: Serials of Illinois Libraries Online—Union List Agency Management." *Serials Review*. 9, no. 2 (Summer 1983): 73-76.

This article describes the development of the *Serials of Illinois Libraries Online (SILO)* union list project. Funded by a 2-year LSCA grant through the Illinois State Library, the initial project created a prototype union list group that would serve as a future model. OCLC served as the computer facility. The issue of centralization versus decentralization is discussed, and staffing considerations, especially the use of student assistants, are noted. Reference notes are included.

Rast, Elaine, joint author.
    See John Tieberg-Bailie
        "Union Listing On the OCLC Serials Control Subsystem."

Rast, Elaine, project director.
   See Serials of Illinois Libraries Online: Manual of Procedures.

Reimer, Diana. "The California State Universities and Colleges Union List of Periodicals." In *Union Lists: Issues and Answers*. Edited by Dianne Ellsworth. Ann Arbor, MI: The Pierian Press, 1982, 23-27.

The California State University and Colleges' Union List of Periodicals (CSUC ULP) contains 29,000 titles and 120,000 holdings records of 19 state colleges and universities. The *CSUC ULP* is not intended to be a bibliographic resource but serves primarily as an interlibrary loan location tool. The article describes the coordination of data collection and input activity in the California State University system. Public service is discussed, and the utilization of the union list is described. Recommendations have been made to shift from a batch mode to an "online interactive system."

Riddick, John. "Serials Automation: Four Years Later." In *The Serials Collection: Organization and Administration*. Edited by Nancy Jean Melin. Ann Arbor, MI: The Pierian Press, 1982, 79-82.

The author describes the OCLC automated serials program at Central Michigan University from 1979 to 1982. The major focus of the article is the format of local data records in an online system.

Riddick, John F. "A Statistical Analysis of the MLC Union List of Serials." *Technicalities*. 5, no. 3 (March 1985): 2+.

This article reports the findings of a study conducted by the Michigan Library Consortium (MLC) with the purpose of collecting data on the "choice of entry and frequency of various fields in the bibliographic record." The MLC union list contains 78,000 titles from 310 various libraries of various types. A primary concern of the study is the projection of offline product costs. Statistical charts are provided.

Rodgers, Patricia M., joint author.
   See Maureen S. Battistella
      "Role of a Health Library . . ."

Rouse, Roscoe. "The Conception and Birth of a Serials List." *Oklahoma Librarian*. 32, no. 6 (November/December 1982); 3.

The author provides a brief historical development of the Oklahoma Union List of Serials (OKULS) since 1967. When the need for currency became a high priority, it was decided to enter union list information into the OCLC database. Funding for project development was through LSCA. The OKULS-3 work was about half completed when a decision was made to contract for the remainder. The contract was awarded to the Pittsburgh Regional Library Center (PRLC). OKULS-3 will contain 45,000 ldrs (local data records) when completed in summer, 1983.

Saxe, Minna. "Going Online With Serials." In *Serials Management in an Automated Age: Proceedings of the First Annual Serials Conference, October 30-31, 1981. Arlington, VA.* Edited by Nancy Jean Melin. Westport, CT: Meckler Publishing, 1982, [31]-41.

The author discusses two interrelated topics: 1) considering several automated systems suitable for serials work, and 2) the feasibility of using any of those systems in serials operations. Ten systems were selected for discussion: Faxon, EBSCO, OCLC, RLIN, UTLAS, WLN, CLASS, PHILSOM, UCLA, and NOTIS. A checklist of questions to consider when choosing a system are included, and bibliographic notes are provided.

Schaffner, Ann C. "Implementation of the Faxon Union List System by the Boston Library Consortium." *The Serials Librarian*. 9 (Spring 1985): 45-62.

A local online union list project developed by the Boston Library Consortium and the Faxon Company is described. The project was funded by a LSCA-III grant and involved 12 academic and research libraries. Record format, data entry, and offline products are discussed. Also attention has been given to editorial review and control, training and documentation, administration and staffing. Preliminary conclusions indicate that BLC will be able to meet special needs and support resource-sharing with the Faxon LINX system.

Schneider, Julia. "The Missouri Union List of Serial Publications: An Update, 1982-1985." *Show-Me Libraries*. 37, no. 4 (January 1986): 14-16.

This article updates previous articles on the Missouri Union List of Serial Publications by Jenny Preston and Sue Burkholder. Since 1982 the MULSP Committee has been reviewing and revising various union list concerns. Results of a user questionnaire support the continued but modified production of COM (Computer Output on Microfiche) and hard copy. Automation improvements are in process, and "an error listing is generated in order to help maintain the integrity of the database." The author stresses the importance of union list maintenance as an ongoing activity.

Schriar, Susanne. "SILO (Serials of Illinois Libraries Online)." *Illinois Libraries*. 69, no. 1 (January 1987): 68-69.

The author notes that *SILO* is in its 3rd phase of LSCA funding and outlines its major uses: location tool, interlibrary loans, serials lists, and access functions. Additional information about *SILO* membership is provided, and offline products are described.

Schwarz, Betty. "Updating PaULS." *Pittsburgh Regional Library Center Technical Bulletin*. (March 1986): 59.

Frequent updating of union list local data records (ldrs) is viewed as a time saving matter for libraries. Up-to-date ldrs enable borrowing libraries to accurately select lenders. Lending libraries can help reduce interlibrary loan requests for items no longer held. Steps for updating ldrs are provided.

Schweitzberger, Kathleen, joint author.
    See Marjorie E. Bloss
        "Guidelines for Union Lists of Serials."

Serial Holdings Statements at the Summary Level: User Guide to the American Standard. OCLC Union List Standards Task Force. Dublin, OH: OCLC, 1983. (OCLC#9889698)

This publication is a user guide. It defines OCLC preferred practice in the use of the standard ANSI Z39.42-1980.

Serials of Illinois Libraries Online: Manual of Procedures. Elaine Rast, project director; John Tieberg-Bailie, technical coordinator; and Carol Feiza, project clerk. DeKalb, IL: Serials of Illinois Libraries Online Project, Founders Memorial Library, Northern Illinois University, [1983], 194 pp.

This union list manual was developed to facilitate and encourage online union list maintenance. The *Serials of Illinois Libraries (SILO)* was funded with an LSCA grant by the Illinois State Library. The manual features a table of contents, introduction, and appendices: 1. Online Participants, 2. OCLC Union List Groups, 3. CONSER Project Participants, 4. Local Data Record Fields and Subfields, 5. MARC Serial Format Fields, 6. Sample Records, and 7. Preferred OCLC Bibliographic Records.

Serials Union List Tapeload Guide. Dublin, OH: OCLC, April 1986. 18 pp.

This OCLC publication is a procedural manual for institutions who may wish to build union list data records by means of a tapeload function. The tapeload guide is designed for programmers, and it sets forth specific steps to be followed when using this method for union list purposes. The manual includes tape requirements, record format, and results of ldrs (local data records) created and not created. Appendices are included.

Settel, Barbara and Tom Gearty. *An Online Union List of Serials: Meeting the User Needs*. New York: Paper presented at the National Online Information Meeting, March 25-27, 1980. (ERIC Document no. 190-053)

This report describes the development of an online database and conversion project undertaken by the Central New York Library Resources Council. Funding from a LSCA grant enabled the 45 participating libraries to create a database through use of the OCLC Serials Control Subsystem. Advantages and disadvantages of the union list project are noted. A user manual and a directory of participating libraries are included.

Shaw, Deborah. "A Review of Developments Leading to On-Line Union Listing of Serials." In *The Management of Serials Automation; Current Technology & Strategies for Future Planning*.

Edited with an introduction by Peter Gellatly. New York: The Haworth Press, 1982, 185-190.

This article provides an historical perspective on the union listing of serials and a discussion of current developments in the area. Bibliographic description is stressed as the essential element of the union list. The feasibility of computer applications in union listing is discussed. CONSER guidelines and ANSI standards are considered. Bibliographic references are included.

Shipler, Virginia. "OCLC, Inc." In *Union Lists: Issues and Answers*. Edited by Dianne Ellsworth. Ann Arbor, MI: The Pierian Press, 1982, 41-45.

This article presents a brief history and use statistics of the OCLC Serials Control Subsystem. The importance of the CONSER project is noted. An outline of the OCLC union listing capability is provided.

Sperry, Timothy J., ed. *Pennsylvania Union List of Serials Procedures Manual*. [1st edition] Pittsburgh Regional Library Center, 1982, 30 pp.

The manual, which was developed in conjunction with the Pennsylvania Union List Project, was intended to assist library personnel in using proper methods of adding and updating union list information and in dealing with interlibrary loans and collection development. Because of changes in union listing guidelines, this manual has been replaced with a new edition (included in this publication).

Sperry, Timothy, ed.
See Pennsylvania Union List of Serials: Core Titles

Stoppel, Kaye, joint author.
See Marilyn K. Nicely
"MAUL: An OCLC Union List of Legal Periodicals."

Strasser, Alexander. *Bibliographic Access in Pennsylvania*. Pittsburgh Regional Library Center. Washington, DC: U.S. Office of Education (DHEW), 1979, pp. 32-34. (ERIC Document no. 171-279)

While at the writing of this report no online union existed in Pennsylvania, the need for broad-based access to state holdings was clearly identified. Establishing an online union list should be a major access priority. Although the impact of an online union list was not clear then, establishing an effective bibliographic delivery system would be needed to facilitate future access.

Sutton, Lynn Sorensen. "Using the OCLC Union Listing Component for a Statewide Health Sciences Union List of Serials." *Medical Library Association. Bulletin of the Medical Library Association*. 74, no. 2 (April 1986): 104-109.

The development of a medical union list as a subset of the Michigan Library Consortium (MLC) list is described. The union list was produced by the Michigan Health Sciences Libraries Association (MISHULS) primarily to serve as a location tool for interlibrary loans. Under MHSLA, an ad hoc union list committee was created to establish objectives and develop a plan of action for union list development. Vendor selection, funding, method of data input, governance, and costs are among the issues discussed. Offline products and ongoing maintenance are noted. Charts, tables, and references are included.

Taylor, David C. "Networks and Interlibrary Loan." In *Managing the Serials Explosion: The Issues for Publishers and Libraries*. By David C. Taylor. White Plains, NY: Knowledge Industry Publications, Inc., 1982, 55-71.

The author provides a good conceptual framework of the relationship between networks and resource sharing. Brief descriptions of the following computerized library networks are included: OCLC, RLG/RLIN, WLN, and UTLAS. Footnotes are included.

Taylor, David C. "Serials Automation." In *Managing the Serials Explosion: The Issues for Publishers and Libraries*. By David C. Taylor. White Plains, NY: Knowledge Industry Publications, Inc., 1982, 73-89.

The author presents a general overview of serials automation from the early 1960s. The advantages of serials automation are presented in contrast to weaknesses of manual systems. Serials automation is viewed as a preliminary stage to an online interactive system. The author concludes by presenting some do's and don't's and problems solved and problems remaining. Bibliographic footnotes are included.

Texas State Library: Library Services and Construction Act. Annual Report. Austin, TX: Department of Library Development, 1979, p. 132 (ERIC Document no. 191-479)

The LSCA Title-III project description of the IUC (Interuniversity Council) of the North Texas Area Cooperative Union List is reprinted. Fifteen academic libraries in the Dallas-Forth Worth area and the Dallas-Forth Worth public libraries will be participating in the online union list of serials project. This first phase will include holding information for 33,000 periodical subscriptions. AMIGOS will serve as the union list contractor.

Thomas, Suzanne L. "OCLC Union Lists On-Line, Using the Local Data Record." *West Virginia Libraries*. 37, no. 3 (Fall 1984): 11-13.

The issue of local union list maintenance by way of OCLC local data records (ldrs) is discussed. The format of the ldr (bibliographic information, fixed and variable fields) and subfields are explained in sequential steps. The author draws upon experiences from the centralized maintenance operation at the University of Pittsburgh. The use of off-line products to cumulate all local union list changes is noted.

Tieberg-Bailie, John and Elaine Rast. "Union Listing On the OCLC Serials Control Subsystem." In *Projects and Procedures for Serials Administration*. Compiled and edited by Diane Stine. Ann Arbor, MI: Pierian Press, 1985, 287-322.

The union list component of the OCLC Serials Control Subsystem contains only five elements: holding library, copy identifier, call number, summary copy holdings, and summary institution holdings. The article describes the procedure for creating an OCLC union list record, and notes the advantages of online access. Numerous illustrations of sample records provide additional clarity and understanding of the union list process. OCLC bibliographic record selection is explained, and the role of ANSI standards is noted. A detailed discussion of management considerations, including anticipated costs, is provided. Footnotes and bibliography are included.

Tieberg-Bailie, John, joint author.
   See Elaine Rast
       "SILO: Serials of Illinois Libraries Online . . ."

Tieberg-Bailie, John, technical coordinator.
See Serials of Illinois Libraries Online: Manual of Procedures.

"Union Listing." In *Serials Control: User Manual*, chapter 9. Dublin, OH: OCLC, 1983.
This chapter provides an overview of the OCLC union listing component and, in typical OCLC style, explains various union list display options and functions.

"The United States Newspaper Program: Cataloging Aspects." *Cataloging & Classification Quarterly*. 6, no. 4 (Summer 1986).
This entire issue contains articles that describe the OCLC Serials Subsystem, including its union listing component and use of AACR2 rules in cataloging newspapers.

Wallbridge, Sharon. "CONSER and OCLC." *Serials Review*. 6, no. 3 (July/September 1980): 109-112.
This article is based upon an OCLC/CONSER brochure which is available from OCLC. Two basic CONSER elements are discussed: authenticating serial records and editing serial records. Standardized practices under OCLC/CONSER guidelines will improve online access and contribute to the overall maintenance of high-grade records in the OCLC database. Cooperation and exchange of bibliographic information between the Library of Congress and the National Library of Canada are described.

Wassenaar, Kathl. "Western Colorado Union List of Serials." *Colorado Libraries*. 10, no. 4 (December 1984): 34-35.
The Western Colorado Union List of Serials (WCULS) project was begun in 1983 with LSCA funding. Project participants were located in three regional systems and included more than 85 libraries. *WCULS*, which contains 12,000 local data records and 4,500 bibliographic records, is administered by the Three Rivers Regional Library Service System. *WCULS* objectives are noted, and preliminary activities are discussed. Plans include a microfiche edition of *WCULS* at the completion of the project.

Weber, Benita M. "Union Listing Activities." In The Year's Work in Serials: 1981. *Library Resources and Technical Services.* 26 (July-September 1982): 285-286.

The major focus of this article is an evaluation of the ALA/RTSD Serials Section Ad Hoc Committee on Union List of Serials and the IFLA Standing Committee on Serial Publications proposed documents on union listing standards. The author discusses the primary reasons for the recent interest in union listing — costs and technology. Both the OCLC Union List Subsystems and the F.W. Faxon Microlinx system are described as examples of online serials databases.

Wecker, Charlene D. and Susan Fayad. "The OCLC Union List Product: Evaluation and Critique of Michigan's Statewide Product." *Serials Review.* 11, no. 3 (Fall 1985): 73-84.

The Michigan Library Consortium (MLC) and the Michigan Regions of Cooperation (ROCs) union list projects are described. Funded by an LSCA Title-IIC grant, the MLC union list project involved Michigan State University, the University of Michigan, and Wayne State University. Both OCLC and RLIN would serve as computer facilities for conversion. As the MLC was getting underway, the Michigan State Library was developing regional networks with LSCA Title-III funds known as ROCs. The authors describe the creation of a statewide union list using the MLC and ROCs databases. Basic tenets for the development of the project are outlined, including governance, cost responsibility, and the option of subsets or statewide groups. Union list issues are discussed, and problems are noted. A union list evaluation form is included.

Wecker, Charlene D., joint author.
See Susan Fayad
"The OCLC Union List Product: Michigan's Recommendation on Design Options."

Whiffin, Jean. "Network/Consortia and Library-Oriented Organizations." *The Serials Librarian.* 4, no. 3 (Spring 1980): 346-347.

The formulation of international guidelines for online union lists is described in this article. The project was funded by UNESCO and awarded to the International Federation of Library Associations and Institutions (IFLA). Both the utilization of computer-produced tools and lack of serials lists in underdeveloped countries support the need for international union list standards. It is hoped that the UNESCO/IFLA project can solidify efforts already underway in the American National Standards Institute (ANSI), the British Standards Institution, the CONSER Project, and the Canadian Union Catalogue Task Group. Project procedures are described. Reader suggestions are requested.

Whiffin, Jean. "Union Catalogues of Serials: Guidelines for Creation and Maintenance, with Recommended Standards for Bibliographic and Holdings Control." *The Serials Librarian*. 8 (Fall 1983): 28-29, 80-82.

An IFLA sponsored project which presents the "complete text of the first draft of the proposed new international standard" for union catalogs is described. Sections 3.3 and 9.7 address the advantages of online systems, display formats, capabilities, and access points. A glossary of significant terms is included.

Wittorf, Robert. "ANSI Z39.42 and OCLC: OCLC's Implementation of the American National Standard Institute's Serial Holdings Statements at the Summary Level." *Serials Review*. 6 (April/June 1980): 87-94.

This article was written following OCLC's adoption of the ANSI standards. It clarifies elements of the summary holdings statement noting variations where permitted. The author emphasizes the importance of selecting correct bibliographic records, explains the entering of summary holdings data, and describes the retrieving and displaying of serial union list information. Illustrations are provided, and bibliographic references are included.

Wolfgram, Patricia A., joint author.
    See Lynn Sorensen Sutton
        "Using the OCLC Union Listing Component . . ."

Woo, Linda. "University of Washington 'Online' Serials Catalog." In *Projects and Procedures for Serials Administration*. Compiled and edited by Diane Stine. Ann Arbor, MI: Pierian Press, 1985, 87-98.

This article describes the background and development of the printed central serials record at the University of Washington, and outlines procedures for updating online records in the Washington Library Network (WLN) database. The University of Washington Library System is made up of several centrally housed collections, the Health Sciences Library, and 18 branch libraries. All WLN participating institutions have online access to the database which is also used to generate COM (computer output microforms). Details are given on the scope, contents, organization of the catalog, and format of entries. Database maintenance procedures are noted. Sample entries and charts are provided.

Woods, Elaine. "Serials: the National Scene." In *Union Lists: Issues and Answers*. Edited by Diane Ellsworth. Ann Arbor, MI: The Pierian Press, 1982, 29-36.

The author provides an overview of union listing efforts, and notes trends and issues that will have an impact upon online union list development. Union list framework will be determined by answering several questions: what is needed, at what level, who reports information, how much information is needed, and what are the levels of responsibility? The use of the MARC format for holdings and locations information will facilitate the online development of serials union lists.

Pennsylvania Union List of Serials: Procedure Manual

(2nd Edition)

Edited by
Suzanne L. Thomas, MA
Henrietta F. Angus, MLS
Alice Bright, MLS

TABLE OF CONTENTS

Introduction

Chapter I. Principles of Union Listing

    A. History of PaULS
    B. Record Selection: Successive Entry
    C. Microform Holdings
    D. Maintenance

Chapter II. Using the OCLC Serials Control Subsystem

    A. Select Options
    B. Viewing Union Lists
    C. Use with ILL

Chapter III. Selecting the Correct Bibliographic Records

    A. Fixed Fields
    B. Variable Fields
    C. Multiple Records

This project is funded under a contract with the State Library of Pennsylvania, Department of Education.

Reprinted with permission from the State Library of Pennsylvania, Pittsburgh Regional Library Center, Pittsburgh, PA © 1987.

Chapter IV. Creating Local Data Records

    A. Fixed Fields
    B. Variable Fields
    C. Standards for Recording Holdings
    D. Editing and Updating Local Data Records
    E. Deleting Local Data Records
    F. OCLC Activities–Merging Records

Chapter V. U.S. Newspaper Project

    A. Background
    B. Bibliographic Records
    C. Holdings Records

Chapter VI. Auxiliary Features in OCLC

    A. Name-Address Directory (NAD)
    B. Offline Products from OCLC

Appendices

    A. Annotated List of Primary Sources for Union Listing
    B. Quick Guide to Bibliographic Records Field Tags
    C. Quick Guide to Local Data Records

INTRODUCTION

This manual was prepared with the support of the State Library of Pennsylvania through a Library Services and Construction Act (LSCA), Title III, grant to the Serials Management Committee of the Pittsburgh Regional Library Center. The manual was written by librarians from member libraries: Suzanne L. Thomas (University of Pittsburgh), chair of the ad hoc PaULS Manual Revision Subcommittee, Henrietta Angus (Robert Morris College), and Alice Bright (Carnegie Mellon University).

The manual was developed to reflect the changes in OCLC union listing procedures and to encourage maintenance of union list information online. The Pennsylvania Union List of Serials (PaULS) is a valuable tool for cooperative sharing of serial resources.

The manual provides basic information about how to select bibliographic records, enter holdings, and use the OCLC Serials Control Subsystem Union List Component. The manual introduces the use of PaULS with ILL and the OCLC Name Address Directory. Information is included about the U.S. Newspaper Project and recording microform holdings.

This manual is not intended to replace any documentation developed by OCLC or the Library of Congress. This introduction compiles basic union listing information with reference to the primary sources and quick guides in the appendices.

CHAPTER I. PRINCIPLES OF UNION LISTING

A. History of PaULS

The Pennsylvania Union List of Serials (PaULS) which began in 1979 with funding from the State Library of Pennsylvania, is an online union list of serial holdings residing in the OCLC database. There are over 250 members in Pennsylvania, with additional participants in West Virginia, Maryland, New Jersey and Delaware. PaULS is a valuable resource sharing tool. It also serves as a record of a particular library or library system's serial holdings. The value of the union list increases with the accuracy of its contents. It is necessary for each participating library to maintain its records to accurately reflect changing holdings information. Every new subscription, title change, cancellation, gift of bound volumes, or ceased title means a change in union list information. Only by regularly updating records will PaULS continue to be useful.

B. Record Selection: Successive Entry

Throughout the manual the use of standards is emphasized. By following the same guidelines for bibliographic record selection and data entry, each participating library can find and interpret records input by other libraries. Choosing the correct records is important when entering holding information. Choose only *serial* bibliographic records.

Sometimes there are several records because cataloging rules have changed and members input multiple records. For the purposes of this union list chose records which reflect "successive entry cataloging" following AACR2 rules. Successive entry cataloging requires that each new title for a serial have a separate bibliographic record. All the union list holdings for a particular title will be linked to the same bibliographic record, not 2 or 3 different records. This is a great advantage for interlibrary loan. Selecting the correct bibliographic records is explained in detail in Chapter III.

C. Microform Holdings

Serial holdings in microform (microfilm, microfiche, microcard, etc.) are reported for PaULS. There are two options for choosing the appropriate bibliographic record used for recording microform holdings.

Option A

Choose the bibliographic record which corresponds to the microform publication. Attach microfilm holdings to the bibliographic record for the microfilm format; attach microfiche holdings to the record for the microfiche format, etc. Microform holdings will be recorded on records for the microform. If an institution holds a title in two formats, the holdings will be attached to two bibliographic records, each reflecting the appropriate format. This option provides complete information about holdings for each copy.

Bibliographic record for hard copy:

LDR SCHD ‡e 4 ‡v 1- ‡y 1917-

Bibliographic record for microfilm:

LDR SCHD ‡e 4 ‡v 13- ‡y 1930-

If there are notes on the local data record about a copy it is clear to which copy they apply. The subscription status code also applies to the specific copy. The holdings information is clearer when it is attached to separate bibliographic records. The disadvantage of this option is that it separates holdings for a single title for the user and ILL. Another disadvantage is the cost of maintaining multiple records.

Option B

Choose the bibliographic record describing the hard copy. Attach holdings for all formats to the hard copy record. Record all holdings in one local data record. The microform holdings are recorded in the note subfield of the local data record. The holdings information is enclosed in square brackets. The type of microform is followed with an equal sign and the microform holdings information. The hard copy holdings are recorded in the same SCHD field using subfields v and y.

SCHD ‡g 0 ‡e 4 ‡n [Microfilm=13- 1930- 0,4]
‡v 1- ‡y 1917-

This means the institution has microfilm for all the volumes published since thirteen and hard copy for volume one to date.

Option B is called "exceptional entry of microform holdings" in the OCLC *Serials Control: User Manual*. The advantage of option B is that all holdings for a title are on one local data record. This collates information for user, ILL and offline products. It is less expensive to maintain fewer records. The disadvantage is the confusion when there are notes on the local data record and the lack of bibliographic description for the microform. Another consideration is converting holdings data.

Option A is the current national standard for recording microform holdings. From 1979 to 1984, while entry of data was centralized, Option A was PaULS policy. Option A is still practiced at some institutions doing their own serials maintenance; however, Option B has been used by all consortia contracting to add their holdings to PaULS. Option B also is widely used by other state and regional union list groups.

While each institution should make an informed decision and have a written policy in regard to the entry of microform holdings on serial records, Option B currently is preferred for PaULS union listing.

D. Maintenance

As stated earlier it is essential that each participating library maintain its holdings to ensure the accuracy of the union list records. Each library should develop a procedure for updating its holdings information on a regular basis. This procedure will vary from library to library. Some libraries catalog serials on OCLC and can incorporate union list updates into the OCLC data input routines for cataloging on a day-to-day basis. Other libraries batch union list activity and update local data records monthly or quarterly. Another option would be to work with an outside source to update union list information on a contract basis.

CHAPTER II. USING THE OCLC SERIALS CONTROL SUBSYSTEM

OCLC's Union Listing Component works within the framework of the Serials Control Subsystem. The Union List Component allows users to view the titles and volume holdings of libraries who participate in a union list groups. (Refer to the *OCLC Serials Control: User Manual*, for more detailed instructions on how to use the subsystem.)

The Local Data Record (LDR) in the Serials Control Subsystem serves as the basis for the Union Listing Component. Holdings information is entered in an online workform called a Local Data Record which is linked to the bibliographic record. The records are designed to be copy specific. A separate local data record is created for each copy of a title held. The OCLC system merges the local data records of many libraries together to form a single union list display. Each library's holdings information displays if that library is profiled for the union list group. The union list symbol for PaULS is PASU.

A. Select Options

Log on to OCLC using a valid authorization number for the Serials Control Subsystem. There are three retrieval options in this subsystem: (1) Online Union Catalog, (2) Union List Group, and (3) Institution. The default option retrieves only those records in the OCLC's Online Union Catalog to which your institution's three character symbol is attached. It is possible to change the retrieval option to retrieve any record in the OCLC database or to limit the search to records used by a specified union list group. This second option retrieves only records which have been used by members of that union list group.

To select a retrieval option:

1. For bibliographic records used by your institution,
enter: *select [your institution's OCLC symbol]* **[display send]**

For example: *selectpit* **[display send]** would retrieve records used by University of Pittsburgh if a PIT log on authorization was used. This select only works for each institution's symbol.

2. For bibliographic records used by a union list group,
enter: *select [Serial Union List Group symbol]* **[display send]**

For example: *selectpasu* **[display send]** retrieves PaULS records.

3. For all records in the OCLC Online Union Catalog,
enter: *selectoluc* **[display send]**

For fast searching when selecting bibliographic records,
enter: *selectpasu* **[display send]**

The search will retrieve only records already used by PaULS members and therefore eliminate some of the duplicate records in the full OCLC database. If this search does not retrieve the correct bibliographic record, search the full database,
enter: *selectoluc* **[display send]**

Edit your institution's LDRs using the select the retrieval option for institution.

B. Viewing Union Lists

Search for holdings in union list groups other than PaULS by using option 2 (above). The codes for union list groups and their symbols are in the Name-Address Directory,
enter: *:ser.* [**display send**]

C. Use with ILL

Local data records from union lists can provide interlibrary loan users with volume specific, summary holdings information. By searching union list holdings, it is possible to determine which specific library within an institution holds the particular volume of a title.

After logging on to OCLC using a valid authorization number for the Interlibrary Loan Subsystem search for the desired bibliographic serial record. At this point, request a union list display for any union list group, enter: *ul [union list group symbol]* [**display send**] OCLC responds with a display including brief information from the bibliographic record and a list of OCLC symbols of the institutions holding the serial and corresponding summary holdings statements. Example:

```
PENNSYLVANIA UNION LIST OF SERIALS
The Journal of human resources
ISSN:0022-166X CODEN: JHREA9 OCLC no. 1604126 Frequn: q Regulr:r
ITEMS MARKED + HAVE FULLER HOLDINGS. REQUEST LINE NO. TO VIEW THESE
        1 + AIB (8608,0,5,0) 4-17 1969-1982
        2 + DXU (8211,0,0,0) 1-2,4-8,10-12 1966-1967,1969-1973,
          1974-1977,1979-
        3   ELZ (8401,0,4) 1-11,17- 1966-1976, 1982-
        4 + EVI (8607,0,4,[Microfilm=v.1-, 1966- 0,4]) 1- 1966-
        5 + LAS (8603,0,5) 13-15 1978-1980
        6 + MRW (8607,0,4,6 Current issues retained
          until microfilm received [Microfilm = 14- 1979- 0,4])
        7 + PIT (8304,0,4) 1 - 1966-
```

The plus sign (+) following a line number indicates that the institution has reported detailed information for its copies of the serial. To view the more detailed information from the institution holdings,

enter: *[line number]* **[display send]**

Example:

```
The Journal of human resources.
ISSN:0022-166X CODEN:JHREA9 OCLC no.: 1604126 Frequn. q Regulr: r
PIT (8304,0,4) 1- 1966-
        1    PIT% (8606,0,4) 7- 1972-
        2    PITB (8603,0,5,6,Retains papercopy until receipt of
             microfilm) 1-8 1966-1973
        3    PITQ (8304,0,4) 5- 1971-
        4    PITS (8304,0,4,6,Retains current year received)
        5    PITT (8304,0,4) 1- 1966-
```

This shows the holdings information for each copy of this title held at different locations at PIT (University of Pittsburgh).

To return to the union list group display from a union list institution display,

enter: *ps* **[display send]**

To return to the full bibliographic record from a union list display,

enter: *bib* **[display send]**

For help using the union list screen displays,

enter: *help* **[display send]**

To return from the help screen to the union list display,

enter: *ul* **[display send]**

For further information see the OCLC *Interlibrary Loan: User Manual*, 3rd ed.

CHAPTER III. SELECTING THE CORRECT BIBLIOGRAPHIC RECORDS

Selecting a serials bibliographic record is the first step in union listing. It is important to have all holdings for a title on the same serial bibliographic record in the OCLC database.

One useful way to search for serial bibliographic records for union listing is to log on to OCLC with a serials control authorization and *selectpasu* [**display send**]. This combination of the authorization and the select command limits all the searches to only records with PaULS holdings already attached. This will eliminate some difficult searches and duplicate records. It is important to remember if no record is located to search using *selectoluc* [**display send**]. to see all the records in the full database.

A. Fixed Fields

```
OCLC: NEW         Rec stat: n      Entrd: 870803                   Used: 870803
Type: a  Bib lvl: s   Govt pub:        Lang: eng    Source: d     S/L ent: 0
Repr:    Enc lvl: l   Conf pub: 0      Ctry: pau    Ser tp: p     Alphabt:
Indx: u  Mod rec:     Phys med:        Cont:        Frequn: q     Pub st: d
Desc: a  Cum ind: u   Titl pag: u      ISDS:        Regulr: r     Dates: 1956-196u
   1    010          LC card number
   2    040          Inputting library codes
   3    022          ISSN
   4    041    0     Language codes
   5    050          LC class number used at LC
   6    082          Dewey class number
   7    090          LC class number assigned by member library
   8    049          Your library's code
   9    110    20    Main entry heading, corporate body name
  10    111    20    Main entry heading, conference or meeting name
  11    245    00    Title ‡b Subtitle
  12    246    00    Various other titles on issue
  13    250          Edition statement
  14    260    00    Place of Publication ‡b Publisher's name
  15    300          Physical description
  16    362    0     Volumes and dates of publication
  17    4XX          Series statements
  18    500          General notes
  19    515          Numbering peculiarities
  20    533          Microform description
  21    580          Title change notes
  22    6XX          Subject headings
  23    700          700-740 added entries
  24    770          772 supplement and main title links
  25    777          787 other related title links
  26    780          Earlier title
  27    785          Later title
```

Bib Level s

Local data records should only be attached to bibliographic serials records. The serial bibliographic record is identified by **Bib lvl** "s" in the fixed field and the square shaped fixed field at the top of the record.

Successive Entry Cataloging

Another critical feature of the fixed field is the s/l **ent.** indicator of "0" for successive entry cataloging or "1" for latest entry cataloging. PaULS has agreed to accept only successive entry cataloging. Latest entry cataloging is unacceptable. This is an important tool for selecting records when serial titles change or multiple cataloging records are available online.

Serial records are often two or more screens long. There are six fields that are important in determining a match. Other fields can provide valuable information about the serial and a quick guide to the fields is in Appendix B.

Fixed Fields to Check

```
Bib lvl:   = s
S/L =      0
Pub st:    c = current
           d = no longer published
Dates:     1987-9999 began in 1987, still current
Dates:     1986-1987 began in 1986, ceased in 1987
Repr:      blank = hard copy  r = reprint
           b = microfiche; a = microfilm
           see related fields 533 and 580
Desc:      blank = AACR1  a = AACR2
```

Institutions vary in their policies in using cataloging that matches the physical format of the serial. The **repr:** for reproduction, i.e., microform or hardcopy of a serial is a critical field for an institution. See Chapter I for a discussion of the holdings options for microforms.

B. Variable Fields

The fields that are important for determining a match to the serial in hand are:

110/710	Corporate name associated with the serial at the time of publication
245	title ‡a main title
	‡e or ‡n section name
	‡f or ‡p part name
260	‡a place publication
	‡b Publisher
362	dates and volumes published with this title
580	note explaining special relationships of earlier and later titles
780	title for earlier volumes
785	title for later volumes

These are the variable fields to compare to the serial in hand. The title 245 must match subfield a and any parts and section names must match. The subfield b is the subtitle and need not match. The 260 place and publication field should match but may be different, check 500 and 550 notes for further information. The 260 field will require judgement to determine if the serial in hand is the same publication when editors or publishers may have changed over time.

The critical field to check is the 362 because the volumes/dates held by the institution are required to fit into the span of volumes/years published. If they do not fit, check the 515 for numbering variations used by the serial. If the holdings still do not fit into the volumes and years given in the 362 check for earlier or later titles in the 780 and 785 fields. The records for these titles are retrieved by the OCLC numbers in subfield 2 or by searching the title. Search the linked titles until the correct record for the title and volumes/dates is found.

C. Multiple Records

There will be times when more than one record matches the serial. The first thing is to check multiple formats by looking at the fixed field REPR and 533 and 580 fields for microforms and reprints. The institution's policy for microform holdings will determine choice of record for holdings.

If the multiple records are all for hard copy, one record must be selected. There are several ways to decide. Always add your holdings to the record with other PASU holdings. This keeps all PASU holdings on one record for interlibrary loan users.

If no PASU holdings are attached to the records or if PASU holdings are on more than one record, check the bibliographic record for the following fields. Is there an 042 field with lc, lcd or nsdp? Is DLC in the second or later positions in the 040 field? Either case would indicate the record was selected for authentication by CONSER libraries and likely to be retained when duplicate records are consolidated by OCLC. If neither situation exists, check for multiple inputting codes in the 040 field for CONSER activity. Check when the first record was entered into OCLC or the one with the most holdings libraries and/or union lists. If none of the above conditions help in record selection, select the most complete record.

Record selection is important in union listing. The quality of the database is improved; there are more serial records available for use and fewer duplicates.

CHAPTER IV. CREATING LOCAL DATA RECORDS

Once the bibliographic record has been selected add the holdings information by requesting a local data record work form: *wf* [**display send.**] A blank local data record (LDR) appears on the screen. There is a fixed field and variable fields. Only the fixed field and three variables fields need to be completed for union listing. Each copy of the title is recorded on a separate local data record. The local data record is edited by sending each line and the fixed field and updating the record when done.

A. Fixed Fields

The most important fixed field is the HLDG LIB, where the four letter OCLC code for the location is input. These codes are the same as those used in the 049 field for cataloging. The system defaults to a four letter code. If there are multiple locations at the institution, the code must be altered to reflect the specific location. This code directs the interlibrary loan requests to the correct location at the institution.

Two other fixed fields may be filled out. Codes are used for SUBS STAT to indicate subscription status at the institution a= active and d= no longer received. LOAN is a one letter code for interlibrary loan policies. Some common ones are "c" photocopy at cost, "a" not loanable. Consult the OCLC *Serials Control: User Manual* for a complete list of loan periods.

B. Variable Fields

The variable fields reflect the location's holdings and the classification number used for shelving of classed serials.

1. Classified serials. If the serial is classified in the institution, record the class and book number in the CLNO field. For Library of Congress class numbers separate the number for subfield b at the last capital letter and any punctuation that may precede it. It is separated in the same way as the cataloging record in 050 or 090 fields. For example: HF5324.V52‡b U54 and ML5‡b .E5683 and Z673.L7 ‡b Y and JX1974.7 ‡b M6 illustrate where to put the subfield b.

Dewey classification numbers are also input into the CLNO field with the book number input into subfield b.

2. SCHD and SIHD Variable Fields. The SCHD field (summary of copy holdings) gives the holdings information for a specific location at an institution and the SIHD field (summary of institutional holdings) gives the combined holdings information for all the specific locations at the institution. Some institutions will have only one location, in which case the specific location is the same as the institution.

The SCHD and SIHD variable fields are related. If there are holdings for the serial in only one location at the institution the two fields will be identical. If there are holdings at more than one location at an institution, the holdings for the specific location (SCHD) may be different from the holdings of the entire institution (SIHD). A full run of a serial may be held in various locations at an institution in which case the SIHD field would be "1-". But the first 10 volumes may be in main library (SCHD "1-10" and the current issues in chemistry library SCHD "11-". There would be a local data record for each location with the SCHD fields reflecting the specific location holdings and one shared SIHD field indicating the institution held the entire run.

If the institution has only one location, the system will process both variable fields as one when a new local data record is created. After the local data record is created, the SIHD field must be updated whenever there is a change in any SCHD field. If there are multiple locations, the SIHD field information must be calculated and input manually. It is not system supplied. The system will edit the SIHD fields of all local data records linked to a bibliographic record, when one SIHD field is edited and that local data record is updated. The system displays the same SIHD field on all local data records linked to the bibliographic record. If one SIHD field is changed all displays of SIHD fields are changed in the local data records.

SCHD Subfields

The SCHD field has six subfields.

‡d = date the ldr was created or updated and is system supplied
‡g = completeness code, use 0 when reporting complete volumes in subfield v
‡f = a nonretention code use blank if the volumes are held indefinitely. If the holdings are discarded or moved to a different location after a period of time, then use 6 and ‡n "retains current year only", etc.
‡v = volumes; use full volume numbers see the ANSI standards for instructions for complicated statements such as multiple series: 1:1-6;2:1-6;3:1-7.
‡y = years associated with the volumes or years of holdings when no volume numbers are on the piece.
‡n = notes about volumes held; use standard terminology for notes from the OCLC Serials Control: User Manual: "Current year retained until microfilm received."

The SIHD field has the same subfields as the SCHD field. The data in the SIHD field represents the holdings for the institution, which must be calculated by the inputter when there are holdings at more than one location.

A method for calculating the institution's summary holdings is to visualize all the holdings for the specific locations brought together on one shelf. Because this is the field that displays for an interlibrary loan user looking for a lender, the ultimate goal is to represent gaps in holdings at the institution.

C. Standards for Recording Holdings

PaULS as a union list group records the holdings according to the *ANSI Z39.44-1986 for Serials Holdings Statements*. OCLC has published a users guide to the earlier edition of the standard: *Serials Holdings Statements at the Summary Level: User Guide to the American National Standard*. These are sources used to resolve recording difficult holdings statements.

PaULS uses the ANSI Standard at level three for holdings, i.e., use complete volumes and indicate gaps. OCLC's current format for local data records indicates usage of option B, i.e., volumes and chronology in separate statements.

Volume Numbers

Union list information is summarized information, not current check in information. Holdings are recorded at the volume level, not the issue level. Only whole arabic numbers are used to record volumes. If the title changes in mid-volume, the whole volume number is recorded. If an institution has at least 50 to 80 percent of the issues of a volume it is included in the holdings.

1. Current Receipt. A dash is used to indicate current receipt of a serial. The SCHD subfield v would be recorded with the number of the first volume received and a dash.

2. No longer received. The holdings are closed with the last volume when the last issues for that title is received or when no more additional volumes will be retained at that specific location.

3. Gaps in Holdings. Gaps in holdings such as missing volumes not held by an institution are indicated by a comma: 1-3,5-7 indicates that volume 4 is not held.

4. Examples. Some examples of recording SCHD subfield v:

Published run	Library Holdings	SCHD +v
v.1-	v.2,no.	2-
v.3,no.3-v.10,no.2	v.3,no.3-v.10,no.2	3-10
v.12-45	v.36-45	36-45
v.1-25,ns.1-	v.23-25,ns.1-	23-25;1-
v.1-50	v.8-15,no.2, v.15,no.4-v18, v.25-50	8-18,25-50

The examples illustrate use of only whole volume numbers using only arabic numerals. Dashes indicate complete volumes between the first and last volumes or continued receipt when no number follows the dash.

Semicolons are used to separate multiple series of volume numbering. If the series is numbered the holdings could be SCHD ‡v8-18;2:1-6;3:1- for a series that published a run: series 1, v.8-18, series 2, v.1-6, series 3, v.1 to date.

Some examples of holdings for multiple locations:

```
Published run v.1-
Location A  v. 1-10                        SCHD ‡v 1-10
Location B  v. 11-15,17-19                 SCHD ‡v 11-15,17-19
Location C  v. 16                          SCHD ‡v 16
Location D  v. 20-                         SCHD ‡v 20-
Composite/institutional holdings           SIHD ‡v 1-

Published run v. 1-16
Location A  v.2,no.1-3, 6-7                SCHD ‡v 2,6-7
Location B  v. 5-10,no.1-2                 SCHD ‡v 5-10
Location C  v. 6-11, 14                    SCHD ‡v 6-11,14
Composite/institutional holdings           SIHD ‡v 2,5-11,14

Published run v. 1-
Location A v.1- (all bound volumes)        SCHD ‡v 1-
Location B Current unbound issues          SCHD ‡f 6 ‡n Retains
current year
Composite/institutional holdings           SIHD ‡v 1-

Published run v.1-
Location A current issues until            SCHD ‡f 6 ‡n Current
microfilm received                         issues retained until
                                           microfilm received
```

Microforms example:
  Published run v.1-
  Location A v.13- hard copy; v.1-12 microfilm

Option A

　Hard copy bibliographic record

　　　SCHD ‡v 13-

　Microfilm bibliographic record

　　　SCHD ‡v 1-12

Option B

　Hard copy bibliographic record

　　　SCHD ‡n [microfilm=1-12 0,5] ‡v 13-

Depending upon the institution's policy, the local data record for the microfilm holdings will be on the hardcopy record or on a separate bibliographic record for the microfilm.

D. Editing and Updating Local Data Records

The holdings information not only must be input the first time an LDR is created but changed whenever the title changes or the location's holdings change. To edit an existing local data record, first search for the bibliographic record and locate the correct local data record. Edit each line that needs to be changed and send each line. Once editing is complete update the local data record. When there are multiple locations, the SIHD field should be checked for necessary edits as well as the SCHD field.

E. Deleting Local Data Records

If no holdings are retained by an institution, the local data record can be deleted from the database. Locate the correct local data record,
enter: *del* [**update send**]

Complete and current information is essential for all users, particularly interlibrary loan.

F. OCLC Activities — Merging Records

OCLC maintains the bibliographic record and the linking of local data records to these bibliographic records. OCLC will delete duplicate bibliographic records from the database and relink any local data records to the remaining bibliographic record. The remaining bibliographic record will have the OCLC record number of the deleted bibliographic records in the 019 field. It is important to check the local data record or records against the new bibliographic record for any necessary correction.

OCLC provides information about these records in the database. Log on to OCLC in the serials control subsystem and request OCLC control #2500016, #10258107, and #10258125.

enter: *ulser* [**display send**]

The display is a list of changes to serial records in the database. Check the list of title changes and merged OCLC records for titles with local data records that need to be changed.

CHAPTER V. U.S. NEWSPAPER PROJECT

A. Background

The U.S. Newspaper Program (USNP) is a cooperative national effort to identify and make available for public use newspapers published in the United States since the 17th century. USNP is funded by the National Endowment for the Humanities in cooperation with the Library of Congress.

The program also coordinates nationally the preservation on microfilm of fragile newspaper collections. Participating agencies are building a national database of bibliographic records and holdings information in the Online Union Catalog. NEH funds have been granted to either national repositories or state projects. State projects are usually administered by a library, an archive or a historical society within the confines of a state. Funding is established initially to plan and promote the project and to identify newspaper repositories within the state. Subsequent grants are made to catalog the newspaper titles and to input data into the Online Union Catalog. The final step in the process is the microfilming of endangered newspapers.

The project in Pennsylvania is administered by the State Library of Pennsylvania. Some 1,400 newspaper repositories, including libraries, historical societies, schools and publishers, have been identified. West Virginia University, which administers that state's project, identified 121 newspaper repositories holding 1,058 titles.

Program participants enter their newspaper holdings into the Serials Control Subsystem. All repositories are profiled as part of the United States Newspaper Program Union List (NEPU). An ILL unit record is attached to each repository's organization record in OCLC's Name-Address Directory for posting the repository's hours of operations and their interlibrary loan policies.

B. Bibliographic Records

The U.S. Newspaper Project uses the master record concept for bibliographic records. This means that holdings are attached to one hard copy record regardless of the format of the holdings. Microform holdings are attached to the hard copy bibliographic record and may not be attached to a microform bibliographic record.

C. Holdings Records

The format of the newspaper holdings records found in the OCLC Online Catalog is different in appearance from the records found in the Pennsylvania Union List of Serials. Originally, angle and square brackets and a special code signifying the microfilm producer were used by USNP to indicate newspaper microform holdings. Currently only angle brackets are used for microform holdings. The holdings themselves are in an issue specific format. Year:month:day is the typical format used. For example,

SCHD ‡y 1952:12:121-31, 1960:3:12-26

The holdings for hard copy and microfilm items are combined on one local data record.

CHAPTER VI. AUXILIARY FEATURES IN OCLC

A. Name-Address Directory

The OCLC Name-Address Directory (NAD) was established in 1980 for the purpose of providing an online environment for the storage and dissemination of information on libraries, vendors, publishers and information organizations. As the name implies, NAD is a compilation of names, addresses and other pertinent information for use in identifying organizations. In addition, the Name-Address Directory provides access to the interlibrary loan policies of member libraries.

1. Organization of File. Records in the Name-Address Directory exist on three levels: an organizational level, a unit level 1 and a unit level 2. The organization level record contains information about the entire institution. Unit level 1 records describe specific parts of the organization such as departments, divisions or offices. Unit level 2 records describe further the departments, divisions or offices found in unit level 1 records.

2. Searching NAD. All authorized OCLC users may create or view records in the Name-Address Directory. If the authorization number is validated for either the full or search mode in the Name-Address Directory, access NAD directly from the Acquisitions, General Services, Interlibrary Loan or Serials Control subsystems. To retrieve a NAD record, precede every search key with a colon (:). The only exception to this rule is when a truncated entry is displayed, select the line number directly without prefacing the search with a colon (:).

Search Strategies in the Name-Address Directory:

a. Name-Address Control Number (NACN). The Name-Address Control Number (NACN) is a unique number assigned by OCLC to each name-address record. With the cursor in the home position,

enter: *:55* **[display send]**

This retrieves the organization record for Robert Morris College Library.

b. OCLC Symbol. OCLC has assigned a unique three-character symbol for each OCLC member library and for each library network. In order to search the Name-Address Directory via the OCLC symbol, end this search strategy with a period (.). With the cursor in the home position,

enter: *:teu.* [display send]

This retrieves the records for Temple University. All libraries participating in Pennsylvania Union List of Serials are profiled by OCLC as members of PaULS and are assigned the code PASU in their organization record.

c. Organization Name. This search strategy retrieves only organizational records. Use the familiar 3,2,2,1 search pattern. Be sure to omit all stopwords found in Appendix A of the Name-Address Directory. For names beginning with the prefixes "Mc" and "Mac", include the entire prefix in the search key. With the cursor in the home position,

enter: *:car,me,un,l* [display send]

This retrieves the organization record for Carnegie-Mellon University Libraries.

For further information on searching the NAD, see the *Name-Address Directory: User Manual.*

3. Exit NAD. To exist the Name-Address Directory, with the cursor in the home position,

enter: *:ret* [display send]

This returns the last display in the subsystem in which the search began.

4. Interlibrary Loan in the Name-Address Directory. In addition to the information contained in NAD, the directory provides a means of identifying all union lists of serials in the OCLC Union Catalog. In order to retrieve an alphabetical list of all union lists, with the cursor in the home position,

enter: *:ser.* [display send]

This retrieves a collective display of the OCLC4- character symbol for all available union lists.

For a display of all Pennsylvania Union List of Serials (PaULS) participants, with the cursor in the home position,

enter: *:pasu*. [display send]

This retrieves a display of all PaULS participants.

The Name-Address Directory also provides pertinent information concerning the interlibrary loan policies of member libraries. The information is usually found in either the organization record for the institution or a unit level 1 record for the institution's interlibrary loan department. The policies often indicate loan periods, renewal restrictions, photocopy charges and non-circulating items.

B. Offline Products from OCLC

Serial Union List Offline Products (SULOP) is designed to provide basic bibliographic information and volume specific holdings for union list participants. Participants have a choice of paper copy, COM fiche or a magnetic tape product. Indexes are available in both paper and fiche format. The indexes lack holdings or location information and refer only to a title and/or the main entry in the union list and the OCLC control number. Machine-readable magnetic tape contains a full bibliographic record and all the union list fields from the local data records.

Semiannually, individual institutions or resource sharing consortia may order from PALINET or PRLC their own subset of the Pennsylvania Union List of Serials.

APPENDIX A. ANNOTATED LIST OF PRIMARY SOURCES FOR UNION LISTING

This manual is intended as a description of the general principles of union listing as done by the PaULS union list group. Following is a list of the primary sources for union listing and serials as done in OCLC.

American National Standard for Information Sciences—Serials Holdings Statement (Z39.44). New York: American National Standards Institute, 1986.

Contains a description of methods to record holdings. PaULS uses summary level 3 for reporting their holdings.

Gorman, Michael, and Winkler, Paul W., ed. *Anglo-American Cataloging Rules, 2d ed*. Chicago: American Library Association, 1976.

Chapter 12 describes the rules for cataloging serial publications. The rules for choosing main entry and determining title changes are 25.5B and 21.2A-C. The rules have been extensively revised and the revisions can be found in the *Library of Congress Cataloging Service Bulletin*.

Serial Record Division, Library of Congress. *Conser Editing Guide*. Washington, D.C.: Cataloging Distribution Service, 1986.

Contains a list of the MARC serial tags and their applications by CONSER members in serial records.

Serials Control: User Manual. Dublin, Ohio: OCLC: Online Computer Library Center, Inc., 1983.

Contains information about the usage of local data records in OCLC for check-in and union listing. The online check-in system is being phased out by OCLC, but the union listing system will remain.

Serials Format. 3rd ed. Dublin, Ohio: OCLC Online Computer Library Center, 1986.

Contains a list of MARC serial bibliographic record tags and their usage for OCLC members and includes OCLC card production information.

OCLC Union List Standards Task Force. *Serial Holdings Statements at the Summary Level: User Guide to the American Na-*

tional Standard. Dublin, Ohio: OCLC Online Computer Library Center, Inc., 1983.

OCLC's guide to using ANSI Z39 with the local data records.

USMARC Format for Holdings and Locations. Washington, DC: Library of Congress, 1984.

This describes the new standard for tags and indicators used for holdings information. This standard will be implemented by OCLC in the future.

APPENDIX B. QUICK GUIDE TO BIBLIOGRAPHIC RECORDS FIELD TAGS

```
OCLC: NEW                    Rec stat: n    Entrd: 870803                  Used: 870803
Type: a      Bib lvl: s      Govt pub:      Lang: eng     Source: d        S/L ent: 0
Repr:        Enc lvl: I      Conf pub: 0    Ctry:  pau    Ser tp: p        Alphabt:
Indx: u      Mod rec:        Phys med:      Cont:         Frequn: q        Pub st: d
Desc: a      Cum ind: u      Titl pag: u    ISDS:         Regulr: r        Dates: 1956-196u
```

1	010	LC card number
2	040	Inputting library codes
3	022	ISSN
4	041 0	Language codes
5	050	LC class number used at LC
6	082	Dewey class number
7	090	LC class number assigned by member library
8	049	Your library's code
9	110 20	Main entry heading, corporate body name
10	111 00	Main entry heading, conference or meeting name
11	245 00	Title ‡b Subtitle
12	246 00	Various other titles on issue
13	250	Edition statement
14	260 00	Place of Publication ‡b Publisher's name
15	300	Physical description
16	362 0	Volumes and dates of publication
17	4XX	Series statements
18	500	General notes
19	515	Numbering peculiarities

20	533	Microform description
21	580	Title change notes
22	6XX	Subject headings
23	700	700-740 added entries
24	770	772 supplement and main title links
25	777	787 other related title links
26	780	Earlier title
27	785	Later title
28	850	NST holding library symbols

APPENDIX C. QUICK GUIDE TO LOCAL DATA RECORDS

Library journal.
Library journal (1976)
ISSN: 0363-0277   CODEN: OCLC no: 2351916   Frequn: s
Regulr: n

Hld lib: DXUS   Copy: Repr: Subsc Stat: Loan: ILL CODE

1 CLNO   Class number ‡b Cutter number

2 SCHD   ‡d 8708 (system supplied)
‡g Completeness code for specific location
‡e Acquisitions status code for specific location
‡f Nonretention code for specific location
‡v Volumes held at specific location
‡y Years for volumes
‡n Notes for specific location

3 SIHD   DXU ‡d 8306 (system supplied)
‡g Completeness code for institution
‡e Acquisitions status code for institution
‡f Nonretention code for institution
‡v Summary of volumes at the institution
‡y Summary of years for institution
‡n Notes for institution

Index

AACR2 Records 4,73-74,115,150
ANSI (American National Standards
    Institute) 12,16,54,83-84,149-152
Administration 8,133,145-146,148
American National Standards Institute. *See*
    ANSI
Automated Systems. *See* Local Automated
    Systems

Bibliographic Access 7,9-10,16
Bibliographic Records 6,65-71,149-150
Bibliographic Standards 14,148

COM (Computer Output on Microfiche) 18,
    25-26,33-34,36,64-65,101-102
CONSER (Conversion of Serials) 4,12-13,
    57,62-63,142,148
Calgon Corporation 121
Carnegie Museum of Natural History 52
Cataloging of Serials 13-14,22,39,61-64,
    73-76,115-116,148-149,203
Centralization 144-146
Collection Development 6,28,88
Computer Output on Microfiche. *See* COM
Computerization in Libraries 97-98
Consortia 129-130,156
Contracted Union List Projects 51-53
Conversion of Serials. *See* CONSER
Copyright 7
Core List 17,20-22,32-34,48,143
Costs. *See* Fee Structure
Council on Library Resources 79-80,95

Databases, Serials 90-93
Decentralization 12-13,17,25,34,50,
    144-145,152,155
Dial Access 49-50,103-104,123
Document Delivery 120
Documents. *See* Government Publications

Exceptional Entry 5,53-54,150-151

Fee Structure 5,57
Finding Tools 28,45,74,89,93-94,107,119,
    146-147
Funding 7,22,29,31-35,41,48,53,78-79,
    132-133,139,152

Government Publications 108
Group Access 43-44,120

Indiana University of Pennsylvania 16,49,
    100,102-104
Interlibrary Loans 15,21,36,51,91,99-102,
    107-109,135-136,154

Keyword Searching 111

LDR (Local Data Record) 98,113-116,123,
    124
LSCA (Library Services and Conservation
    Act) 132,155
LTA. *See* Library Technical Assistant
LVAIC (Lehigh Valley Association of
    Independent Colleges) 52,129-130
LVAIC Union List of Periodicals 130-131,
    135-136
Latest Entry 72-73,109
Lehigh Valley Association of Independent
    Colleges. *See* LVAIC
Libraries, Growth & Development 97-99
Library Services and Conservation Act. *See*
    LSCA
Library Technical Assistant 116
Local Automated Systems 7
Local Data Record. *See* LDR

MULS (Minnesota Union List of Serials) 4,
    62

Maintenance 6-8,13,29,32,34,41,48-51,
    56-57,100-101,124-127,143-145
Medical Libraries 4
Microforms 76,134
Minnesota Union List of Serials. *See*
    MULS
Motivational Issues 154
Multiple Data Records 4,64-66

NJULS (New Jersey Union List of Serials)
    154-155
NYCON (New York Consolidated Union
    List of Serials) 155
National Serials Data Program 10
National Data Base 142
Network Environment 141-143
New Jersey Union List of Serials. *See*
    NJULS
New York Consolidated Union List of
    Serials. *See* NYCON
Newspapers 46,110,157
Non-OCLC Members 27,43-45,144

OCLC Database 4,74,93
OCLC Serials Advisory Committee 5,75
OCLC Union List Capability 15,29,43,46
OCLC Union List Format 101-102,147-150
Offline Products 44,56,64,116-118,121,
    126,135-137,144-145,150,152
Online Access 29,110-111
Online Databases 90-93,104

PALINET (Pennsylvania Library Network)
    10,54,142,147,153-154
PRLC (Pittsburgh Regional Library
    Consortium) 11-12,16,19,22,37,54,
    60,67-71,143-144
PRLC Spring Conference 50,53
Pennsylvania Library Network. *See*
    PALINET
Pittsburgh Regional Library Consortium.
    See PRLC

Quality Control 134,145

RFP (Request for Proposal) 10-11,20,133
RTHD Field (Retrospective Holdings) 11,
    64-66

Reference Service 102-104
Request for Proposal. *See* RFP
Regional Cooperation 107,156-157
Regional Resource Sharing 120-121
Retrospective Conversion 115-116

SPIRES (Stanford Public Information
    Retrieval System) 111-114
Serials Cancellation Project 45,56,81-88
    Benefits 85-86
    Description 81-82
    Workshop 84-85
Site Locations 13,49
Special Libraries 11,24,28,119-120
Staffing 13,39,49-50,103
Standards 82-84
Stanford Public Information Retrieval
    System. *See* SPIRES
State Library of Pennsylvania 9,14,19-20,
    25-26,156
Subfields (*see also* RTHD) 64-65
Successive Entry 4,74-75,109

TCLC (Tri-State College Library Consortia)
    25,28,32,156
Technical Issues 148-152
Training 8,144,147,152-155
Tri-State College Library Consortia. *See*
    TCLC

U.S. Newspaper Project 5,45,211-212
Union Library Catalog of Pennsylvania 142
Union List Benefits and Uses 6,63-64,74,
    143,146-147
Union List Conversion 35-36,66,132,
    134-135,145-146,149-150
Union List Goals and Objectives 63-64,
    133-134
Union List Maintenance. *See* Maintenance
Union List Manual 6,54-55,123,144,
    193-218
Union List Participation 121
Union List Problems 4,38-42,55-56,146,
    150
Union List Procedures 123-127
Union Lists 94-95,100
University of Pittsburgh 13-14,27-28,35,
    47-48,144

University of Pittsburgh Files 4, 62, 66-69

WVNET (West Virginia Network for Educational Telecomputing) 111

West Virginia Board of Regents 111

West Virginia Network for Educational Telecomputing. *See* WVNET

West Virginia Union List 108-110

West Virginia University 52

West Virginia University Libraries 115-118

Workshops 147-148

For Product Safety Concerns and Information please contact our EU representative GPSR@taylorandfrancis.com
Taylor & Francis Verlag GmbH, Kaufingerstraße 24, 80331 München, Germany

www.ingramcontent.com/pod-product-compliance
Lightning Source LLC
Chambersburg PA
CBHW060603230426
43670CB00011B/1953